Janet
- just
Here
you enjoy it -
Hope enough
of the class will
be back -
Sincerely, June

by
June Lyman

# DON'T TAKE AWAY MY PASSPORT

by
June Lyman

MANCORP
PUBLISHING

P.O. Box 21492
Tampa, Florida 33622

"To my husband, Harry, and my daughter, Sally, for their support."

June Lyman



Typesetting: JA Studios

Cover design: JA Studios

Printed in the United States of America

**Library of Congress Cataloging-in-Publication Data**

ISBN 0-931541-27-1

# CONTENTS

# INTRODUCTION

# INTRODUCTION

Why do we travel? Is it to escape our humdrum lives? To rise above every day minutiae? We all need a fresh perspective and a good look at the world around us. It doesn't mean we must go far away, just somewhere we haven't been in a long time, or ever.

Richard Haliburton in his book, *The Royal Road To Romance*, tells of his many remarkable adventures including swimming the Panama Canal, and like the mythical Leander, the Dardanelles between Europe and Asia. Haliburton often quoted Oscar Wilde, "Don't squander the gold of your days, listening to the tedious or giving away your life to the ignorant, and the common. Live! Live the wonderful life that is in you."

Other travel writers have inspired us: Burton Holmes, Osa and Martin Johnson, and Harry Franck. Their tales of fascinating trips have whetted the appetites of many a would-be traveler, including ourselves.

This book about our adventures (and mishaps) is for the armchair traveler and anyone else interested in new experiences and in ways to make that next trip more enjoyable. Each adventure is a challenge, a chance to learn more about people and the world.

In *Don't Take Away My Passport,* I hope our enthusiasm for traveling will give new impetus to those off on another trip and enable those who stay at home to share our experiences.

# 1

# THE TEN COMMANDMENTS OF TRAVEL

*Harbor in St. Thomas, 1970.*

# THE TEN COMMANDMENTS OF TRAVEL.

In the lounge of the Norwegian freighter, the *M.V. Salvador* there is a plaque on which is engraved the Ten Commandments of Travel.

THE FIRST COMMANDMENT

*"Thou shall not expect to find things as thou hast them at home; thou hast left thy home to find things different."*

One hot summer my uncle offered us rent-free his rustic cabin in northern Wisconsin. It was in the depression, and there was no money to take a vacation. However, we managed to scrape up enough cash to fill the gas tank of our old touring car, so we made the trip. I was as excited as the children when we strapped our suitcases and groceries on top of the car, piled in with our collie, and headed north.

We weren't prepared for primitive living. Even our small daughter balked at carrying water from a well some hundred yards from the cabin, but after the first day, we all took turns. Another chore was collecting wood for the cook stove. None of us had ever used an outhouse before, and this one was some distance into the woods. It took real courage to go out there at night, amid hoots from the owls, and to risk meeting some wild animals.

It was a simple vacation spent in the outdoors, taking long walks through dense forest, breathing deeply of the pine, gathering blueberries and wild flowers, and later lying in the porch hammock reading. Swimming in the cold spring-fed lake was great, but how we shrieked when our bodies made contact. Nothing ever tasted any better than that fish just caught and fried with bacon, and corn on the cob picked that morning by a neighboring farmer. Evenings we played rummy in the dim light of a kerosene lamp, and when we went to bed, we had to be careful to draw the blanket that served as a partition between our bedroom and the children's.

That vacation made us realize the best things in life, God's world of natural beauty and serenity, are free. Our way of life was reduced to the bare essentials that month, and we had a wonderful time. Since then our family has taken many trips, but our children speak most about that summer in Wisconsin.

Recently we traveled in New Zealand where the language is the same as ours with a few variations and the culture similar, but some of the customs are surprising.

We were taking a train from Dunedin to Picton, bound for the North Island. The hotel manager in Dunedin suggested we use Mt. Cook Air ("Much better than the train, sir.")

He seemed genuinely distressed when we chose the railroad, saying we wanted to see the countryside.

The train was a surprise: a diesel engine, a baggage car, and two coaches. There were only four passengers in our coach. The lady who sat just behind us began a conversation. She had just returned from Scotland. By the time we reached our first stop we had learned her husband had been killed in World War ll, and that she lived with her two daughters.

After two hours, our train slowed.

"Why are we stopping here?" Harry asked, leaning out of the open window. I noticed a small restaurant beside a lake. By now the engineer and conductor had left the train and gone inside.

Our new friend stood up and said, "There won't be a buns' rush today." Then, seeing our puzzled expressions, she went on to explain sometimes when there were many passengers, everyone hurried to buy buns, creating a crush.

"But is this a depot?" Harry asked. "Everyone seems to be leaving the train."

"It's a stop for tea," Margeret said, "and a chance to talk about what's going on."

When we went inside the coffee shop, the engineer and conductor were having a spirited talk about the lambing situation. Because of low temperatures, conditions were very favorable for ninety percent of the lambs to survive. The engineer spoke about the lack of storage and the possibility of having to kill some ewes because of this.

The man sitting at a table near us said he was in the "slink skin" business and that it was very quiet. Margeret later told us that he collected dead lambs' skins.

We climbed back on the train after a refreshing half hour of tea, buns, and conversation, wishing we had such a custom in the states. Can you imagine our harassed businessmen taking time out for such a break?

Later when we took a bus tour through the South Island, a group of Americans had come into our hotel just before us. The innkeeper was shaking his head and sighing. "Oh, you Yanks. Why aren't you like the British? When they climb off the bus, they ask, 'Where's our room?' But what do you say? 'Where's the ice?'" The New Zealanders could not understand why we ruined our whiskey with ice. Although there were refrigerators in our various rooms, no ice tray was ever provided.

THE SECOND COMMANDMENT:

*"Thou shall not take anything too seriously, for a carefree mind is the beginning of a fine vacation."*

Have you ever left home and on the way to the airport wondered if you left the stove turned on or if you locked all the doors? I call this "going away jitters", and it happens to me almost every time I'm off on a trip.

Friends who visit us often leave suitcases and garment bags in our guest room closet, then call from the airport just before their plane is leaving to ask us to bring them their luggage even though we live fifteen miles away.

Recently our neighbor called us frantically, saying his most important suitcase had been left in his front hall. As he would be away two months, it was imperative that it be found and brought out to the airport. Harry and another neighbor went into his house, but found no sign of his luggage. Just as he boarded the plane, he sent word that he might have left it in his closet. On searching further, they found the suitcase there, its airline tags attached. Harry took it to the airport to put it on a later plane. Later we learned our neighbor didn't receive his bag until he reached Tahiti.

Not long ago, while we were waiting for our plane, I found my book of travelers' checks was not in my purse. We called our neighbor who had our house key, and she located it on our kitchen counter. Since Harry had his travelers' checks, we told her to put mine in the desk, as it might take a long time for a package to reach us.

Once you leave home, you tend to forget your fears and not to worry. Sometimes you have no control over what might happen to your property, anyway. Once while we were away our basement became flooded when an emergency pump failed to operate after an unusually heavy rainfall. Luckily, Harry's father lived next door and was accustomed to water in the basement of his old house. By checking ours, he discovered the faulty pump and replaced it.

If one thought of all the terrible things that might happen, he or she would never leave home. Misfortunes happen even if you stay home. The best way to avoid nervousness about leaving is to have a check list. One for packing necessary items like sturdy shoes and a raincoat, another for medications and extra pairs of glasses or contact lenses, and so on. Another list is for daily schedules for mail to be held at the post office unless our absence is to be longer than a month (in this case we ask a neighbor to collect it), for someone to be engaged to mow the grass, and for a friend to pay monthly bills when we're away for a long time. Since we live in close proximity to our neighbors, they watch our house. One will go in and check everything once a week. In return, we do the same for them.

We leave our itineraries with our children, neighbors and friends. At the last minute, we check our passports, driver's licenses, credit cards (with facsimiles), and travelers' checks.

Confident all is in order, we are then able to leave home and enjoy our vacation.

## THE THIRD COMMANDMENT

*"Thou shall not let other passengers get on thy nerves, for thou are paying out good money to have a good time."*

It's unfortunate, but some people are born complainers. Conditions for travel are seldom perfect.

Often the weather can be rainy, cold, or extremely hot. The bus may break down, and another one will be a long time in coming.

On our way across Morocco from Agadir to Marrakech, it was dusty and hot. Our bus was old, and after an hour, the temperature suddenly grew very uncomfortable. The air conditioning had failed. Omar, our guide, began to open the windows, letting in hot air.

"What are you doing?" screamed the woman across the aisle from me. "Do you want to cook us to death?"

Omar, a small, gentle Moroccan, said, "But I am only trying to bring fresh air in. What you Americans call 'air condish'."

The woman stood up in the aisle wringing her hands. "Can't someone do something?"

Her husband pulled her into her seat. "It won't be long before we're there. Look at those beautiful Atlas Mountains while I fan you." He valiantly waved his travel folder in front of his wife.

When we got off the bus and went into a restaurant for dinner, it seemed even hotter. The same complainer called loudly for a martini. To our surprise, the waiter nodded and soon came back with a bottle of Rossi's Martini Vermouth. I can still hear that woman cry, "I want gin!" We felt sorry for her husband.

The show of the evening featured "belly dancers". Plump young girls swayed from side to side, chanting, "Ya, ya, ya." The disappointed men in our party groaned. Our complainer, ignoring Omar's explanation that these were country girls who had never performed before, cried, "Where did these girls come from?"

THE FOURTH COMMANDMENT

*"Remember thy passport so that thou knowest where it is at all times, for a man without a passport is a man without a country."*

A passport is a formal permission given by a government to a foreigner allowing him to pass through that country. As everyone knows, our passport is written by the State Department and identifies us as U.S. citizens. In some foreign countries, passports are hard to obtain, and not everyone has the freedom to travel abroad as we do.

Recently friends who had just returned from Madrid told of a harrowing experience they had had in the railroad terminal. Betty's purse was seized by a vagrant, who disappeared before her husband, Bob, could give chase. In her handbag were their passports, driver's licenses, travelers' checks, and credit cards. They had to wait a long time at the U.S. Embassy before any identification could be given them. Betty advised us to have xeroxed copies of all our important documents, including our passport. "And don't buy any over-the-shoulder handbags. It's much better to hug your purse so that nobody can possibly snatch it," she advised.

The next year when we vacationed in Spain, I remembered Betty's advice and had xeroxed copies of our passports made. Since crime is rampant in cities like Seville, we got in the habit of leaving our passports in the hotel safe and carrying the copies with us. To our surprise, we found that banks would even cash our checks when we presented our passport facsimiles.

We became so accustomed to leaving our passports behind in the hotel, that we were unprepared for a situation in which our copies would not be acceptable.

From Torremolinos on the Costa del Sol, we took a bus to Gibraltar, expecting to spend the day sightseeing with our Grand Circle group. At the entry gate, a security guard climbed on board and asked for passports. Realizing this was one time we would need our real passports, Harry looked at me. Sure enough, the guard scowled at our copies and shook his head, directing us to get off the bus. Our friends groaned in sympathy as we left. In another moment, the bus had disappeared through the gate leaving us on a dusty road with no houses nearby.

THE FIFTH COMMANDMENT

*"Remember to take only half of the clothes you think you need and twice the money."*

If we are off on a tour to Europe or the Far East taking planes, busses, and trains, we each carry one bag, sturdy soft sided , twenty inches long, thirteen inches wide, and eight inches deep. This one suitcase fits under an airplane seat, on the rack above a train seat, and very easily in the trunk of a small foreign car. Best of all, we can each carry our own suitcase from the turntable to customs and on to a connecting bus and another airline terminal. Our luggage can't be left behind or lost because it's with us.

However, it takes practice and thought to pack enough clothes to keep us clean, comfortable, and attractively dressed for all kinds of places and occasions.

What shall we pack? Pack the basics first: a toilet case filled with small-sized packages of cosmetics, medicines first aid supplies, and soap powder, a complete change of lingerie, plus extra panty hose, a pair of soft knit slippers and a light robe. (Often in English or European hotels, a private bath is not always available.) Usually I take just one extra pair of shoes, somewhat dressier than the sturdy walking shoes I wear en route.

My total wardrobe, including what I wear on the way, adds up to two skirts, a pair of slacks, two jackets or a jacket and warm cardigan sweater, six tops (shirts, turtlenecks, or pullover sweaters ranging in dressiness and warmth), a swimsuit, two dresses and a knitted wool vest. It's important to mix match the skirts, tops, and jackets. I like hats for dress and also to shade my face from the sun, so I bring a wide brimmed straw and pack around it.

Since we usually travel in the summer, most of our clothes are washable and drip dry. A clothes line with inflatable hangers and snap clothespins is a must, and thin plastic bags are good for stowing damp laundry. Airlines or tours often supply travel bags that are good for carrying reading material and a camera. Harry leaves his electric shaver at home, taking instead a razor and shaving cream. He has a cosmetic bag for his toiletries. Like me, he coordinates his two pairs of slacks and two jackets with a slipover sweater and T-shirts. One good dress shirt with a tie for formal occasions and two sports shirts complete his wardrobe along with two sets of pajamas and a light robe. He wears his walking shoes and takes along some for dancing. His airline bag will hold his camcorder, film, and a sports cap.

The above packing is considered for trips by plane, train, and tours. In another chapter I will speak of packing for a freighter voyage or a cruise where it's possible to unpack for a long period.

We carry three international credit cards – Visa, MasterCard, and American Express travelers' checks, and before we leave home, we make arrangements for funds to be wired from a cash account to the foreign bank nearest us. As for money, it's important to have more than you expect to spend because in traveling, many unforeseen events can happen. An accident, sudden illness, bad news from home making it necessary to cut short a trip can all be distressing, especially if you find you are short of funds.

## THE SIXTH COMMANDMENT

*"Remember if we were expected to stay in one place, we would have been created with roots."*

If we stayed at home, think how little we would know of the world and its people. I feel travel enriches one's appreciation of life. It's fine to be content with one's own heritage, even proud of it, but with travel, our eyes are opened to other cultures and we have a better understanding of things and people foreign to us. It took many years of travel to make me realize my own culture was just one of many.

When Peter Jenkins started his journey and later wrote about it in *A Walk Across America*, he had many prejudices about the south and black people. The same is true of all of us. It is particularly hard to overcome ideas transferred from our parents to ourselves. My mother had a strong aversion to anything foreign. She had never traveled abroad, yet treated the young immigrant girls from Ireland and Germany who did housework for us with great kindness.

THE SEVENTH COMMANDMENT

*"Thou shall not worry; he that worries has no pleasures. Few things are fatal."*

A friend was crossing the Atlantic on the *Queen Elizabeth* 2; she had read about the *Titanic* and seen the movie *Poseidon Adventure*, in which a giant ship struck a reef. As their ship neared the Grand Banks of Newfoundland, where the *Titanic* had hit an iceberg, Marion grew more and more nervous. The

*Queen* needed refurbishing, and she was sure something tragic was going to happen on this trip. In the middle of the night, there was a great crash. Marion jumped out of bed, flung herself on her husband crying, "I knew this would happen. We've struck an iceberg!" Walter awoke with a start, and leaped out of bed. He went to the porthole but could see nothing. Then passing the bathroom, he paused. "Here's what we heard - the ceiling of our bathroom has fallen! I told you this ship needed repairing."

Some people are afraid of becoming seasick and of being on a ship when there's a bad storm. Others are sure their plane will crash. Travelers on a long motor trip worry about drunken drivers and being killed on the highway. All these things could happen, but every day, even at home, you are at risk. There are remedies now to prevent seasickness, motorists drive more defensively, and commercial jets have good safety records.

THE EIGHTH COMMANDMENT

*"Thou shall not judge the people of a country by the one person with whom you have trouble."*

Last summer a young Spanish student visited us for a month. He came over with twenty classmates under the auspices of the Spanish department of our local high school. It was soon evident that he had been eager to escape the restraints of his wealthy family and have a good time in the U.S. with his Spanish friends. He was not interested in us, or our family. He sniffed at Harry cutting our lawn. "Our servants do that," he said. He chafed under a curfew and at not being allowed to drive (his father had just bought him a new Mercedes). We gave up our own plans to chauffeur him about, and helped other hosts entertain the group. Some were nice young people, but our José was a taker. When he returned home, he did not write us a thank you note or acknowledge the album of film I sent him. This experience left us with a bad feeling toward all Spaniards.

Two years later we were traveling in Spain. Our train entered Seville just as a storm struck. When we got off, there were no porters, and we had more luggage than usual, because we were to be away two months. The grandson of a lady Harry had helped onto the train seized our luggage and told us to follow him. To our surprise, he stowed our gear in a small foreign car. The boy's father was driving, and his grandmother sitting beside him had my suitcase on her lap. They motioned for us to climb in back with the boy and his sister. At our hotel, the father opened the door for us, bowing low, then took my hand and kissed it. You can imagine how we feel about Spaniards now.

THE NINTH COMMANDMENT

*"Thou shall not make thyself too obviously an American; when in Rome, do as the Romans do."*

The "ugly American" image was ever in our thoughts when we spent a month traveling about England. We chose an English touring company, based in London and so economical that no Americans, except us, chose it. The differences between the British and ourselves were marked. In fact, we delighted in comparing the ways they spoke, and attitudes.

As our bus left London and entered the lush countryside of Devon, a large Englishman across the aisle told us of his good fortune. He had just acquired some land and was now a squire. Proudly he stood up, pointing to the scenery ahead. "I say, isn't this superb?" he exclaimed. We suppressed our impulse to laugh. None of the other passengers even smiled. Their companion was just echoing how they felt about their country's beauty.

Later we stopped in a small town for tea. While Harry wandered about taking photos, I sat on a rock and sketched an old inn. When we climbed back on the bus, an older man who had been talking with us said, "Have you and your missus had a spat?"

Surprised, Harry shook his head. "We do our own thing. Junie does pen and inks, and I'm a camera buff." Later we thought of the English couples who had walked, hand in hand, into the inn for tea. None had separated as we had.

At another stop that day, we climbed back on the bus and were asked, "Where are all your parcels?" We told them we were on a budget like they were and had little extra money for gifts. Most of them shook their heads in disbelief. Their picture of Americans had been drawn from movies and TV. All Americans were wealthy and traveled to shop.

In Polperro, Cornwall, our hotel room was unusually large. "This is great," Harry said. "Now let's see about the beds." We both require firm mattresses because of bad backs, and this had been a problem with modest accommodations. Harry threw himself on our double bed and found the mattress sagged so that he hit the floor!

Did we complain to the management? No! Long before this trip, we had vowed to never act like the "ugly American". That night we pulled our mattress onto the floor and slept there. Imagine our surprise the next morning when we found most of the tour passengers, all English, had moved across the street to a better hotel.

We learned a lot about the British, and, in turn, we gave them a different picture of middle class Americans.

> THE LAST COMMANDMENT
>
> *"Remember, thou art a guest in every land, and he that treated his host with respect shall in return be treated as an honored guest."*

During our Elderhostel stay in Sogndal, Norway, we exchanged many ideas with our young Norwegian instructors. Imagine our embarrassment when one of our group bluntly asked, "How does it happen that a nation as intelligent as yours should choose a socialistic system?" We all hissed, and no more was said.

Keeping in mind the above commandments, we participate in a mutual acceptance of different cultures. There is little thought of being with "foreigners". We try to be tolerant of those who travel with us, and keep an open mind, presenting a positive American image abroad.

# 2

# THE MASTER PLAN

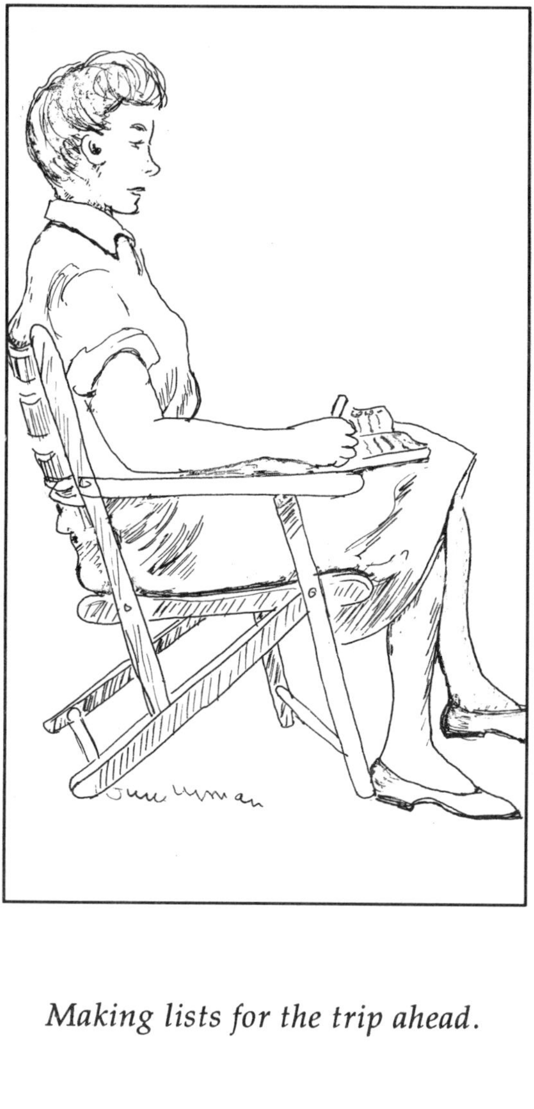

*Making lists for the trip ahead.*

# THE MASTER PLAN

Half the fun of traveling is reading brochures about interesting places and then deciding what is most appealing. AAA's *Going Places*, *Travel Tips* (freighter travel), Condé Nast *Traveler*, and Fodor's *Europe* and *Caribbean* are books that will fire your imagination to explore. Added to these are cruise brochures that arrive by mail daily inviting you to see the world.

Traveling in foreign countries requires planning and taking care to have documents needed to enter certain countries. Are our passports current? If not, we'll need to visit our local courthouse and apply for an extension. Luckily, although the fees have gone up, passports are now valid for ten years.

Some countries require visas or endorsements made on a passport to allow entry into the country visited. This statement testifies that the passport is in order, thus permitting a visit for a limited time for a specific purpose (in this case, visiting as a tourist). When on a freighter, the country's embassy must be contacted, but on cruises, a travel agency handles the visas needed. Brazil is difficult to visit, because the time in which the visa is valid is limited.

It's important to arrange credit before leaving home. The major credit cards like Visa and MasterCard are honored the world over as are American Express checks. A record of the checks' serial numbers, date, and location of the national bank that issued them, should be kept in a suitcase in case the checks are lost or stolen. Local charge cards should be left at home, preferably in a safety deposit box. Several times I had mine in a "secret place" that I forgot. It wasn't until six months later when all my cards had been replaced that I found the original in an old scarf box I seldom opened.

Many foreign stores will accept personal checks (as long as you can produce a Landing Card from your ship) giving a better price than on a credit card. It's usually better to exchange U.S. dollars for foreign currency upon arrival. Cruise ships will exchange our money for another country's but often cannot convert it back to dollars. Local markets will only accept cash. Usually it's wise to have ten or more single dollars. However there are times when a country will not accept any American dollars.

In Capetown, South Africa, there was no time to exchange our money into rands before taking the cable car up Table Mountain. At the summit, it was unusually warm. I ordered an orange drink at the concession but when I gave the man a dollar he shook his head. A man beside me handed him a coin and gave me the drink. I offered him my dollar, but he just smiled and said it was a pleasure to treat me. He introduced himself and said he and his family had just flown in from the Transvaal to celebrate Easter. His wife and children joined us outside, and for a few minutes, we talked about the states and about how glad we were to see their country.

Did you know that Medicare isn't valid outside the U.S.? It's important to carry travel insurance that covers last minute cancellation of a trip. This also includes doctor's bills for illness or injuries incurred on the trip and for lost luggage. There are so many ways to hurt oneself! Sometimes I am admiring the scenery and forget how uneven cobblestone streets can be. Luckily I have sustained only minor bruises and sprains. Climbing off and on a European bus with its high steps can be dangerous, and walking at night around a ship's deck, I fell over a ventilator cover. How many automobile accidents occur on unfamiliar roads? Driving on the left hand side of the road can also be a hazard, especially if you drive at night.

Before we leave home we visit our doctor and dentist. Cards include our blood types, current medications, allergies, eye prescription for glasses or contacts, and date of immunizations. For our world cruise, the public health nurse suggested we have five shots for polio and meningitis (there was an epidemic in Bangkok), tetanus, yellow fever, and cholera since we would be visiting so many third world countries. To our surprise, some of these injections are expensive and are not covered by Medicare.

We pack a first aid kit, nose drops, pills for diarrhea, sunscreen, spray anesthetic, hot water bottle, and a heating pad. On large cruise ships, toiletries are available, and on freighters, little is carried beside aspirin. Film can be expensive, if bought abroad, and video film is hard to find.

Before deciding on a specific trip, read the brochures carefully, noting details and exactiy what costs are involved.

Do you have a tour director, and will he stay with you the entire trip? Has someone from the travel agency taken the tour recently and checked it out? Are there additional travel benefits not included in the cost?

If taking a cruise, decide which shore excursions appeal to you in interest and cost. Many overland trips are optional but require additional shots as well as money. On a freighter, the Line arranges for shore trips and pays for them.

As a general rule don't sign up for an overland tour until you're under way. When we arrived in Singapore, it was very hot, and I had twisted my ankle on the previous shore excursion. How glad we were we had signed up only for the morning tour! Our ship imposed a stiff penalty if you canceled a tour you had previously committed yourself to take.

If in this country, leave your telephone number with your travel agent. Traveling any distance on a ship makes contact more difficult. In case of death or a serious illness, word will be sent through a travel agency or cruise line agent.

It's important to carry extra copies of everything including your birth certificate, tickets, visa, passport, and credit cards.

Most important of all, plan to go where you want to go! Friends and relatives may recommend a trip they loved, but it might not be your taste.

Bargain rates look great, but are the tours more reasonable because it's off season, and weather is either too hot or too cold? On the other hand, there will be fewer tourists. So we must choose between off-season prices and ideal weather. If the altitude is high, as in Machu Picchu, Peru, Harry would be miserable. He is uncomfortable even in mile-high

Boulder, Colorado. A trip to the Galapagos Islands sounds glamorous, but a friend found she wasn't able to climb from rock to rock without someone helping her.

We ask our travel agent how much physical exertion is required on a certain trip. A quick tour of Europe can be very strenuous because not enough time is allowed to rest. Climbing off and on sightseeing buses requires stamina and good knees. So much whirlwind traveling can be confusing, too. One lady we met at Victoria Station told us her week's tour was a blur of cathedrals, palaces, and museums. She couldn't even remember in which country they were and was so tired she longed to go home. My grandmother traveled widely and once gave me some good travel advice: "When you see a ladies' room, use it. When there's a chair in any public place, sit down. If you find a couch, lie down."

After we decide where we're going next, we visit the library and read about the country's location, history, and government. Its natives and development are important, too. If there's time we often take a beginning course in the language. It helps to know basic things like "Hello" (*Jambo, Buenos dias*) "Where is the ladies' room?" (*Ou sont les toilettes pour dames*?) "Where is my hotel?" (*Wo ist mein hotel*?) We always carry a small dictionary that not only translates English into a foreign language, but translates that language into English.

At times, though, trying to make oneself understood can be frustrating. In Switzerland, our small European hotel had several nationalities among its employees. Only one spoke English, and the first morning when we ate breakfast, I could not make anyone understand that I wanted a soft boiled egg. A kind Yugoslavian lady came to my rescue. She spoke Hungarian to our waitress, and finally my egg arrived.

When a destination has been chosen, find a map of the city and locate where you are staying. Are the points of interest nearby, so that you can walk to them? Or must you use public transportation or a taxi?

A good hotel manager, the concierge, earns his tips. He is the source of all knowledge from directions for the underground to the best restaurants (not the most expensive, but those with the best food and service).

Small hotels can often be an adventure. Foreigners are apt to use them. The concierge often has a better chance of finding theater tickets, and although the distance from the city's center is often farther, there will be less noise and confusion. One convenient small hotel near Victoria Station in London is Ebury Court popular with Australians and New Zealanders.

Whatever we do or wherever we go, we'll have to have energy. This means when we embark on any trip, we must be in top physical shape. Because I have a bad back, I try to walk regularly. Before a trip I try to increase my distance working up to five miles. Since our house has no stairs, we look for some to climb whenever possible, keeping in mind those steep steps on foreign busses. Freighters often don't have elevators, and the slippery ramp to climb aboard the ship requires sure footing and stamina. A friend, planning a trip to China, found a park that had many steps leading up to its monument. Fred climbed the hill and long stairway once a day for a month before he left for the Orient. He was anxious to explore the Great Wall and knew walking along it required special fitness.

Most tour representatives will caution those with limited physical ability about certain trips that require agility and energy. On elderhostel programs, cross country skiing is described as a "physically active" course. Others described as schools of outdoor education at high altitude and cold are designated "for outdoor oriented active elderhostelers". This preparation before a trip makes us able to follow a guide or take a walking tour of an ancient city.

Each of us wants something special from a trip. Not all our tastes are the same. Bill and Alice visited Bermuda after we had been so enthusiastic about the island. As soon as they returned, we couldn't wait to ask them how they liked St. George, steeped in history. "We didn't have time to go out there," Bill said. "We found a couple at the Belmont who liked to play golf, so that's what we did every day." They went to Scotland and played the course at St. Andrews, not caring about Edinburgh's history or exploring the highlands.

Have you noticed there are some people who don't have to leave their hometowns, but, through reading and watching travelogues, seem knowledgeable about the world? These are the same people who know who founded their hometown, where the the historic landmarks are, and that an Andrew Wyeth hangs in their museum. They can also tell you the best restaurant in town, and where you can find the best Bed and Breakfast. These same interesting people can describe rafting down the Colorado, or skiing in Snowmass, Colorado.

I hope these friends who are "aware" do travel, because what treats they will discover because they already know so much.

On the other hand, there is Bart Hanson, who stopped at Niagara Falls on his way east. "I don't know why people rave about all that water- such a lot of noise" he said. "And when we took the boat under the Falls, we got all wet. If some guy was going over in a barrel, it might have been worth it."

Or a woman on one tour saying to me, "Thank the Lord our guide speaks the language here. I wouldn't want to be alone in any foreign country."

Usually someone speaks English, but if you have to communicate in an emergency, there's always a way to express yourself.

One of the most stressful afternoons we ever spent was in Italy. Our freighter, *The Zvir*, had docked in Naples at 8 a.m. When we left, the purser reminded us the ship sailed at 6 p.m. If we failed to return in time, it would be necessary to fly (at our own expense) to Salonika, Greece where the ship would be in a week.

Because Harry had never visited Italy , I planned to take him by bus over the exciting coastal drive to Amalfi. By 8:30 we set out on a large air conditioned bus filled with Sunday tourists. It wasn't long before we discovered busses of all nationalities were also determined to travel on the same road, some ill equipped to navigate their superliners around the sharp turns. One wrong decision might mean death on the rocks hundreds of feet below. Our Italian driver stopped more than once to help a German or Dutch driver in distress. It was clear the three hour trip would stretch to five hours or more. By the time we reached Amalfi, it was 1:30 p.m. only four and a half hours from our ship's departure.

Instead of a relaxed luncheon in a café overlooking the Mediterranean, we would have to return on the next bus. It was due in a half hour. We hastily devoured pasta bought from a vendor while we waited nervously for the bus, already ten minutes late.

A ceramic bowl nearby was just what I wanted, so I entered a shop to pay for it leaving Harry at the bus stop. When I came outside, he had vanished. Frantic, I looked about, thinking I had only a few lira, and no passport or identification.

Then came a shout-more like a scream. Looking down the road, I saw a man half off a bus, waving his arms wildly. It must be Harry! I covered the two blocks faster than the time a bull chased me on our farm. Harry caught my arms and dragged me onto the bus. All the passengers cheered as one, *"Viva l'amore!"*

Harry is usually a mild man, but now he was eloquent. Gradually, his story unfolded. The bus driver had been behind schedule so he just let Harry hop aboard and continued on his route. Harry spoke no Italian so resorted to his not too fluent French. *"Monsieur, arrêtez! S'il vous plait. Ma femme est là"* pointing to the station he had left. The driver shrugged and kept on going. *"Attendez, monsieur! Arrêtez!"* He beat his chest in despair. One glance at him, and the driver stopped the bus. That's when

Harry leaned out and gave such a yell that everyone within earshot was startled.

Even so, it was unlikely we would reach our ship in time. I showed the driver a sketch of our freighter and underlined 6 p.m. above it. He nodded, understanding our dilemma. When the bus stopped at Sorrento, he motioned for us to get off, making a diving motion with his arm. *"Metropolitano,"* he said.

"Subway," Harry cried. We were lucky to board a train just leaving for Naples. It was 6:15 when we arrived at the dock. To our immense relief, our ship was still there.

Many times a tour guide will interpret and speak for the passengers. But sometimes it is a real adventure to find out about a native, even using pidgin English, or a smattering of his language, to communicate. Natives are eager to try their English, however limited it may be. Once in a Yugoslavian market, a man came up to us, grinning. "Chicago," he said proudly. All we could do was return his smile and nod.

It's important to set forth with an open mind, not expecting anything but to see different scenery, meet interesting people, and enjoy varied menus.

Sometimes preconceived ideas of how we imagine things prove false. How disappointed I was when we arrived in Marrakech, Morocco, and found the city is now so large that reaching the Sahara would take many hours. I had counted on seeing camel caravans cominq in from Timbuctu. But in Agadir, a Riff came racing over the hill, spurring his camel onward just like Lawrence of Arabia. That was worth stopping in Morocco.

The Polynesian islands, especially Tahiti, have lost some of their initial charm because the girls wear blue jeans, and everyone rides a motorcycle. But in more remote places like the Celebes, the natives wear leis and grass skirts. Tonga, the last Polynesian kingdom, seems relatively unspoiled. The native boys climb the tall palms for coconuts, the women weave tapa cloth and dance the traditional *Lakalaka*. The men join in this singing poetry, truly a memorable spectacle.

When planning a vacation, it helps to have a purpose. There are train buffs who travel by rail only and go to areas where steam trains have excursions. A friend who collects antiques visits the Pennsylvania Dutch country looking for treasures. My brother is intrigued with historic markers and finds Maine his favorite state, especially Castine. Widows I know love to play bridge and prefer cruises where they can play duplicate. Well known artists lead groups to their favorite painting grounds and have workshops. There is a cruise ship now featuring music from symphony to jazz.

Almost any kind of trip will inspire photographers. Now many have camcorder video cameras and return home with videos of wherever they have been. Our slides are gathering dust, but once in a while we show them and delight in scenes we've forgotten. Still, it's much easier to slip a film into the VCR and watch on television the saga of one's travels.

I always take snapshots to put in an album, a wonderful reminder of a trip, and old fashioned as it sounds, I keep a diary. I am reminded of something Oscar Wilde wrote. "I never travel without my diary. One should always have something sensational to read on a train."

# 3

# FROM DECKHAND TO DECK CHAIR

*Cruise ship, Royal Viking Sun, in the Maldives, 1991.*

# FROM DECKHAND TO DECK CHAIR

Where can a tourist become a part of the crew? On a barefoot cruise sailing through the West Indies.

This no frills vacation on a windjammer is popular with men because the only clothes needed are blue jeans, a T-shirt, and a bathing suit. Women must expect few comforts, and must help hoist the sails and stand watch at night.

For those of you who have not had this experience, I relate some of the events on our schooner, *The Flying Cloud*. Our daughter, Barbara, had persuaded me to take this trip. "You'll really love this life, Mom," she said. "No cooking, no telephones."

Climbing the rope ladder onto the ship was a test I barely passed. In the lighted saloon, passengers were sipping rum swizzles. Men outnumbered the women five to one. To my surprise, most were my age. Wasn't this a trip for young people?

Our cabin opened out on deck. Babs explained the foot high ledge across our doorway kept water from coming in during rough weather.

To my relief, she claimed the top bunk. I took off my shoes, noticing how swollen my ankles were from the heat. My feet would need a lot of toughening for me to enjoy going barefoot.

Too tired to unpack, we flung ourselves onto our bunks but found it much too hot to sleep. Through our open portholes, laughter drifted from the saloon. It was a swinging crowd, all right.

At breakfast, the man across the table said, "You're not like my wife. She only likes those big luxury cruises." A shout from a passenger announced the arrival of freshly made rolls. "Enjoy the pastry while you can," our fellow passenger said. "We won't have any under sail."

Afterwards, we went up on deck where everyone gathered in the cockpit, shielded from the sun by an awning. Instead of deck chairs, long kapok-filled pads were stretched out for lounging. A man lying nearby looked up. "This is where I'm going to sleep. It's too hot and crowded below." We learned there was a dormitory type cabin for single men.

*The Flying Cloud* began to move under auxiliary power past yachts and fishing trawlers to the open sea. The volcano, Mt. Pelée, on Martinique was barely visible above the rain clouds. Our schooner began to roll.

Babs and I had just made ourselves comfortable on pads when the captain gave orders to hoist the sails and clear the deck. All the pads were rolled up and stowed in the stern. Passengers and crew formed a line to pull up the main sheet. Soon our sails ballooned and carried us along at a fast clip.

The swells became larger and with increased speed, the schooner began to roll and pitch. A few hardy passengers had returned to their pads, intent on watching the white caps and deep troughs between waves. The rest of us took refuge in the cockpit aft. At swizzle time, everyone went below. Some of us, unsure of our footing, crawled to the companionway. Halfway down, I saw the sea was splashing against our cabin door.

As the sea listed to port, and water ebbed, we made our way to our cabin. Our suitcases were floating in two inches of water. Babs helped me pull them onto my bunk. Thank heavens the clothes inside were dry. We and three other passengers came to dinner.

Our ship must have dropped anchor during the night for the next morning two young black men grinned down at me from the dock above. "You want taxi, m'am," one called.

Shaking my head, I hastily closed the door.

After breakfast, everyone was told to go up on deck. The captain, an Englishman, would tell us about British St. Vincent. A small man in white, he talked about the natives, a mixture of Portugese, negro slaves, and East Indian coolies. It was clear he knew the islanders well and had great affection for them. He also had a sense of humor. "We sail at 1:00 a.m. tonight," he said. "If you miss the ship, meet us in Grenada. We'll be there in a week." The crew had told us the captain had no fixed itinerary and never took roll call. I looked at Babs who was always late, but she was more interested in the next announcement. A steel band would play for us that night at a nearby inn.

Everything the captain said about St. Vincent was true: the rare tropical plants, Cannonball trees, and giant Traveler's Palms, banana plantations, and fields of arrowroot. We even ate baked breadfruit, which was delicious!

A high point was snorkeling at Sandy Island. The chief engineer led the way to show us the spectacular underwater garden.

Saline Island, noted for its shells, attracted the collectors. Babs and I went ashore but found the tangle of sea grapes along the beach made walking impossible. Only the discovery of an unusual West Indian Fighting Conch compensated for the concentrated attack of no-see-ums.

That night it was my turn to stand watch, aided by a crew member. The stars formed a bright canopy, and all was silent except for water lapping against the hull, and people whispering as they brought up blankets and pillows to sleep on deck.

The first glimpse of Grenada's warehouses and gabled houses reflected pink and blue in the still harbor was memorable. Such a peaceful setting for so many blood baths between the Carib Indians and the French, then the French and English, and more recently our own stand against the Cuban communists.

On the beach boats were turned, so that their bottoms could be scraped (*careening* this process is called). We sniffed the fragrant nutmeg on our way up the hilly streets to St. George, flattening ourselves against the ancient walls whenever a car passed. The policemen directing traffic from platforms were in enviable positions.

That night after dinner, a small group of musicians boarded our ship. They were neighbors of the crew who lived on the various islands we'd visited.

It was easy to sense the West Indian rhythm . The crew intermingled with the passengers making it very lively. The whole ship seemed to sway with the beat. Some of the popular American tunes the native boys had learned by listening to old records. Our bare feet hurt, but we kept on dancing.

Sailing on the next day the water became so shallow that we could see coral reef just beneath the surface.

Suddenly the man at the helm shouted, "Captain!" We saw the ship's wheel spin out of control, and the captain with the aid of two men swung back on course. "Never came across a whirlpool in here before," he said.

Just then our lookout turned and motioned for the captain to reverse course. A jarring tremor shook the ship, then the order came to drop anchor. We had struck a reef. Later the crew dove repeatedly under our bowsprit. (Our steward said they were looking for lobsters.) Before dinner we learned a hole, the size of man's fist, had been made in the hull. The crew had caulked it temporarily as the men in the hold manned the pumps to get rid of the bilge water.

Everyone knew our second lifeboat was out of commission. Only the day before, as the boat was being lowered during a drill, the line broke, and it fell into the sea. The stern broke up as it struck the water, and soon bits of wood drifted away on the current. What was left of the boat was stowed on board until repairs could be made at our next port of call, Bequia.

That night our ship limped along on auxiliary power. Not even the champagne the captain ordered for dinner helped relieve the passengers' anxiety.

The next morning sounds of hammering awoke us. Our ship was anchored a few yards off shore where scaffolds and ships in dry-dock cluttered the beach. Bequia!

Later, a builder showed us how he cut white cedar with his adz. The boat he was working on had been ordered by our captain the year before. The heat was so intense that most of us sat on the patio of the Hotel Frangipani where later we had a lobster dinner. Passengers were allowed to dive off the ship. Until then, strong currents had prevented anyone from swimming. I, too, joined them for a better look at the figurehead, a buxom lady in gold.

After a stop at Pigeon Island, so called because British Admiral Rodney used to keep pigeons there, we set sail for our home port, Martinique. Despite heavy seas, a few passengers went out in the launch to photograph our *Flying Cloud*. After eleven days, everyone was tanned and fit. Some of us had even lost weight. The men had grown full beards. This had been a special kind of trip. Our schooner had been small enough to sail into out of the way ports. Our captain knew all the places we visited so intimately we had been well received by the natives. We had explored places not often visited and in waters so clear that fish seemed an arm's length away.

If you're adventurous, are not prone to seasickness, and want a no-frills vacation, this is for you!

We have found that by taking all kinds of transportation travel can have a third dimension. In marked contrast to a Barefoot Cruise, booking passage on a large luxury liner is another type of adventure.

Probably the most popular type of travel today is taking a cruise. The time may vary from three days, a short trip where the emphasis is on gambling, to a long one over a hundred days that involves a large ship sailing around the world with thirty-two or more ports of call. The latter may be taken in segments of a month or less.

Recent statistics from Condé Nast show that only one thousand people in the U.S. take cruises over a month long. The majority prefer a cruise of one or two weeks.

Why do people prefer shorter trips? The following reasons might account for this: restlessness "How can I stay on a ship so long; I'd feel trapped;" reluctance to leave business or property for a longer time, fearing he will lose money in his absence or his home might be burglarized; health reasons, why he shouldn't leave his doctor for a long period; cost, a longer cruise is often more than the average person can afford; or length of vacation, unlike Europeans, the American often has only a one or two-week vacation.

The above reasons make Caribbean cruises popular. They are short, and leave and return to Miami, Florida. West Indian ports are colorful with good shopping and interesting sight-seeing. Such trips are usually inexpensive.

Many, like the one my family and I took on the *Boheme* are planned for every age, especially the children. Horse races, costume night, bingo, and floor shows are some of the events all enjoy. The *Commodore Line* ship has special rates during the summer for families and senior citizens.

Why are cruises so popular? Some people dislike flying. It's great to unpack and know you can store your suitcase until you reach your home port. The majority are especially interested in food and entertainment. To relax and to enjoy twenty-four hour room service appeals to many. Your fare includes all meals, transportation to all the places you go, and varied diversions. The package includes air or bus fare to and from the port. Also, there is greater informality on short cruises.

Ship lovers find life at sea a great adventure. Watching a pilot help guide a large liner to port can be fascinating. After a shore excursion, sailing away to the island's band, and throwing streamers to the crowd on the dock can be very exciting.

On a ship the cuisine and service is like a five star hotel's. You will have the opportunity to meet and share experiences with hundreds of different people. You have the choice of participating in many activities or being left alone to relax and enjoy your privacy.

There are some small ships like Cunard's *Sea Goddess* and the Royal Viking's *Queen* that accommodate about two hundred passengers and are small enough to sail into ports that cannot accommodate the larger ships.

It is important to decide what you want from a cruise: a rest, a chance to see interesting countries, and participation in sports. Entertainment varies with emphasis on floor shows, athletic events (an Olympic tournament was held on our ship), casino nights, dance classes, classical music, and enrichment lectures about the culture of the country visited.

The size of a ship determines whether there are two dinner sittings, early or late, or just a single one. An early sitting leaves little time for a cocktail hour, but means the entertainment will follow dinner, so that you can retire early. The second sitting allows for cocktails, and a later floor show. The cruise price is an all inclusive package that covers meals, floor shows, the ship's facilities like the exercise room, the swimming pools, and the theater.

A passenger on a tight budget may find costs have gone up since he last traveled on a cruise ship. Alcoholic drinks are expensive ($3.30). As a result, more passengers are buying liquor at ports of call and having the happy hour in their cabins. Laundry and dry cleaning, beauty shop service, and visits to the ship's doctor are extra expenses, and cost much more now, so do shore excursions of two or more days. To keep track of what you are spending, it's a good idea to check your bill weekly. Then the total sum owed at the end of the trip will not come as a shock.

Is the cabin you have chosen in a good location? On our ship there were a few cabins that are inside at the minimum cost. This is the best value since meals and entertainment are the same as for a deluxe accommodation. However, only three percent are classified "minimum", and they sell quickly. It's wise to study the ship's deck plan, and to decide if you'd be happy in a small cabin without a porthole or window. These low cost accommodations may be economical on a week or ten day cruise, but for longer ones, you may want more room and a view.

It's best to make your dining room reservations in advance. If you do, a card with your table number will be in your cabin when you embark. How many people do you wish at your table? Four? Eight? Or do you prefer to dine alone? Word has it that a table for four can be risky, should you and the other couple be incompatible. Friends we know never take a chance on strangers, but prefer a table for two. However, a table of eight can be stimulating, and there usually are some passengers you will like very much. It's a good idea to change tables once a month if you are on a long cruise. Dinners are lengthy, and conversation can run thin after a long time together.

As long as one knows everything about the ship he chooses, rates, itinerary, service, and reputation (much traveled friends praise the good cruises including service and food), he can be relatively sure he won't be disappointed in it.

The cruise industry is very competitive. There are special interest or theme cruises that appeal to certain people. Some ships specialize in bridge tournaments where addicts can earn master points; others have lectures on high finance; opera fans can sail on a cruise "Music Festival at Sea". There's an "Inside Washington Cruise," and even Shakespeare is featured on several voyages.

Shore excursions can be expensive. Sometimes, if you have already visited a port, you won't need a tour but can explore on your own. Recently, visiting Cozumel, we went to our favorite beach, rented snorkeling gear, and snorkeled most of the day right off shore. Some ports are easily accessible, and there is no need to get on a sight-seeing bus. Many times one can get the flavor or atmosphere of a country just by walking along the main streets and watching the natives .

We do not like to shop, but never cease to be fascinated by local displays of handwoven goods and colorful vegetable and flower stands. Choose shore excursions carefully before signing up. There are expert consultants on your ship to help you.

Your travel agent and folders from the cruise line may urge you to sign for certain shore excursions before you sail. These are often not refundable. It's wise to wait and see how you feel and whether the weather is favorable before paying for a shore trip. Overnight overland tours can be very expensive, and one needs to know how strenuous the tour will be before signing up.

Most land tours consist of morning and afternoon tours, or an all day excursion. Transportation in the Pacific is generally by bus, many of which are old, and have poor springs and narrow seats. The best seats are usually in the front and midsection. The worst are in the rear. All passengers want good seats, so there is a rush to be first on the bus. Despite the shore excursion manager's appeal to wait for her first call to board, passengers are off the ship as soon as the gangway is lowered. There often is no air conditioning, so the test of a good traveler is to be uncomplaining even though uncomfortably warm.

Some people will not sign up for a cruise because they're afraid of gaining weight as their friends have. Dr. Abraham Friedman, author of *Fat Can Be Beautiful*, gives advice on how a cruise ship passenger can enjoy gourmet delicacies and not gain weight. He says to eat slowly, savoring each morsel, and take small portions of delectable and exotic food. Another way is to skip a meal, no breakfast, or no lunch. Dr. Friedman does advise omitting the midnight buffet.

What to wear? Life aboard a cruise ship is relaxed and informal. For daytime wear, slacks and various bright colored tops are the rule, but evening calls for long skirts or a dressy pantsuit. The ship's daily paper will let you know what sort of dress is required that night, formal, casual or informal. Formal means a tuxedo for men and dressy pants or long gown for ladies. Informal means cocktail party clothes and casual means slacks or jeans with no jacket or tie for men.

For formal wear most men prefer white dinner jackets because they are cool. On a long cruise, two jackets adding different cummerbunds and jabots for variety appeal to men. Since long dresses are no longer in fashion, short sequined gowns are popular. However, many seasoned travelers pack finery only reserved for cruise wear, and this usually includes long gowns. Glittery gold jackets are now worn, not only for show but for warmth. Most ships are air conditioned and in the evening, one feels comfortable wearing a shawl or jacket.

Shopping is important on any cruise and one of the purposes of shopping is finding some unusual shirt or skirt characteristic of native wear and promptly worn for the duration of the trip. There are not many bargains now, so finding a special buy creates a furor among the ladies. Sometimes one has only to look at the gay hats worn by travelers disembarking to know where they have visited.

All cruise ships have doctors, one or sometimes two, to handle medical emergencies. It's wise to consult one if you've sustained an injury to your knee or foot. Be sure your teeth are in good condition, because there are no dentists. Also take a good supply of prescription medicine with you, for these ships carry only a limited amount. Keep your doctor's bills: your insurance covers them under a clause in your Cancellation Policy.

Important to pack are comfortable walking shoes. Even evening slippers should have low heels because you may be dancing when the sea is rough. More and more, the wardrobe trunks of yesteryear are returning. They can be sent directly to the ship. And, if you are returning later on for another cruise, they may be stored on the ship. In the newer ships, there are walk-in closets that will accommodate many changes of costume.

VCRs are in cabins, allowing anyone with a camcorder movie camera to see his videos. Closed circuit television informs passengers about the ship's location and daily schedule. There are interviews of interesting people aboard.

No longer does anyone at sea need to feel cut off from the world. Communications by satellite keep one informed about events around the globe. It is easy to telephone anywhere from the ship.

Because of world conditions, security is tight. Close watch is kept on those entering a cruise ship. Even passengers must show their identification and landing cards when they return from an excursion ashore. The man in charge of our ship's security once was in charge of the Queen of England's safety. Careful check is made of parcels and luggage with radar scans similar to those at airports. While in port, guards patrol and even use frogmen to be sure nothing has been attached to the hull. Friends wishing to come aboard to visit must apply for passes long in advance of the sailing.

Those who use cruises as a way of life have certain ships they prefer. They even return to the same cabin trip after trip. As a result, the liners that have the best ratings are usually full.

Most people find this way of traveling not only relaxing, but enjoy the luxury of fine service and excellent meals. It's no wonder that new ocean liners are being built every month to meet the demand of the traveling public.

# 4

# BY RAIL

*Steam train rounding the bend, 1938.*

# BY RAIL

My first train trip was in 1928 when my father took me along on a business trip from Chicago to Los Angeles. The *Southern Pacific* carried me from a small Midwest town out into the world of adventure and gave birth to a desire to travel that has never left me.

My grandfather, C.C. Secrist, had been a railroad man and had helped develop the *Pacific Fruit Express*, which had the first refrigerated railroad cars. As I sat on the rear observation platform, I felt part of the train, too. I remained out there most of the day and early evening, fascinated by the rapidly passing scenery - rivers, prairies, mountains, watching the shadows deepen, and the sparse towns become lighted as we sped through them. I can still smell the cinders as they flew up from the railroad bed, and hear the choo-choooo of the steam engine as it climbed the steep grades. When the train chugged around a bend, I could see all the cars. As the small stations were left behind, canyons ahead formed a dark tunnel through craggy purple rocks. The loneliness of the plains and desert seemed like the end of the world. The memory of sitting on that open observation car, watching the track going back will always be with me.

Even though I was thrilled to see Hollywood and get Douglas Fairbanks' autograph, I was eager to climb aboard the train again and take my place on the observation platform to watch herds of buffalo and elk along the tracks.

Instead of listening to my adventures, my mother was more concerned with the coat she'd made me. No longer beige, it was now black with soot. My father only shrugged and said he was glad I loved traveling on a train as much as he did.

In the fifties, streamliner observation cars had rounded ends with loveseats facing the rear, but this was not like being outdoors to hear the sounds and to enjoy all kinds of weather.

Many railroad memorabilia can still be found. The private cars once owned by railroad presidents and millionaires are now being collected and restored by train buffs. My grandfather's had a sitting room, two bedrooms, dining room, kitchen and shower. A genial attendant always made special desserts when he knew I was coming aboard. Cabooses are now bought to be used for guest houses or for a place to exhibit model railroad trains.

A railroad fan will travel far just to take a short excursion on a steam train. These runs, like the one on the Green Mountain Railway from Bellows Falls, to Chester, Vt . and from Scranton to Moscow, Pa. are popular. Scranton is now the site of Steamtown, a National Park. Such steam locomotives as the *Union Pacific's* "Big Boy", the *Nickel Plate's* "Berkshire", and the *Boston and Maine's* "Constitution" can be seen, as well as a railway post office car and a caboose. Nearby, the restored Lackwanna train station has been made into a hotel by Hilton.

As Michael Palin says in his *Around the World in 80 Days*, a trip taken in 1989 in which he used only ship and train to circle the globe, "If I fly, I won't see a thing." People who have the time and inclination prefer train travel. Some have a fear of flying, while others, like those who take the Autotrain from Sanford, Florida to Lorton, Virginia, prefer to break up a long automobile trip by going by rail because of comfort, entertainment, and the reduced chance of accidents.

Amtrak still is plagued with delays caused by the breakdown of old equipment and tracks, but both service and food is improving. The smiling porters and luxurious dining cars are a thing of the past, but the latest extra fare trains promise even those will be back.

It is unfair to compare Amtrak to European trains because the latter are subsidized by the country's government, which is dependent on railroad transportation to move large masses of people from one city to another.

One has only to recall the *Orange Blossom Special* (withdrawn in 1953) with luxuries like a club car with a barber, a ladies' lounge with a boudoir, specialized service with porters and dining-car waiters wearing armbands with the name of the train embroidered in silk, and even air conditioning (1934) and diesel power (1938) to realize what comfort we once had on our trains.

When we board the *Silver Meteor* and the *Silver Star* on the Seaboard Railway, we are riding in trains that are the descendants of the grand railroads of the past. These runs, because of their popular southern destinations, are still popular and continue to prosper.

Train travel make you alert to things of the past; the railroad stations in the south still are reminiscent of separation of blacks and whites, having two sets of tickets windows, waiting rooms, and drinking fountains, all used until 1960.

Amtrak has been beset with three problems: they don't own the railroad lines, freight is more profitable, so it has priority, and the equipment is ancient with carriages thirty years old and electric locomotives fifty years old. No wonder it seldom runs on time!

Amtrak (the National Passenger Railroad Corporation) runs most railroad passenger service throughout the country. The good news is it has replaced daytime equipment between Boston and Washington with brand new stainless steel Amfleet passenger cars. One of the most successful runs is the *Coast Starlight* from Seattle to Los Angeles. This express serves every major college on the West Coast. Although the train is well equipped for comfort, it does not attract the carriage trade who save time by flying. I hear that if you wear a jacket and tie to dinner, the only other person in the dining car so dressed will be the steward, now called Lead Service Attendant. Customers no longer tip as they once did when the porter brushed your coat and helped you from the train. Once traveling by train was the only way to go but, now you have to be old, a railroad buff, or a tourist to cross the country by train.

Recently, writer Ludovic Kennedy took the *Broadway Limited* to Chicago where he stayed overnight, and he then proceeded west on the *San Francisco Zephyr*. The ticket cost $309.50 to cover over 3,000 miles. The route from New York to Chicago was the same taken by the crack *Twentieth*

*Century Limited* forty years ago. I remember it well, for it took me back and forth to college. My classmates and I usually had upper berths because there it seemed less likely we would have an unwelcome drunk from the club car bother us.

Once the *Zephyr* began rolling west, passengers started to relax, and enjoy one another. Someone played an old fashioned upright piano in the club car.

During World War II, I recalled how lucky I felt to have passage on the old Union Pacific from Chicago to San Francisco. The train was overcrowded with women and children sitting in the aisles, but because my baby was only four weeks old, I had a small roomette. My army husband was anxious to see his daughter before he was shipped overseas. Unable to go to the diner, I found a vendor, who came on at some small town, and bought sandwiches.

Some of the stations now lead double lives. The Union Station in Ogden, Utah uses its main concourse for Saturday night dinner dances, as does the Lackwanna in Scranton, Pennsylvania. The Union Station in Chicago is still a hub of railroad travel, especially since the old Dearborn station is gone.

What Amtrak now needs is new rolling stock and modernized tracks like the ones on the east coast. The long distance passenger trains are at risk because freight has the priority; it's more profitable. Today, you can't be sure when your train will arrive, and many colorful towns like Cheyenne, Wyoming are no longer stops.

In spite of this lack of equipment, Americans are beginning to enjoy train travel. In fifteen years Amtrak has increased its number of passengers, and people are taking much more interest in railroads. James Jerome Hill was the founder of the *Great Northern* railway from St. Paul to Puget Sound in 1880. He is remembered by all those who have ridden the *Empire Builder* as the pioneer who opened the northwest and, especially, the wonders of Glacier Park. Today's train is unlike the Pullmans and custom built domes of thirty years ago, and there is no china in the diner or glassware in the club car, yet, as it descends the western slope of the Rockies, it reveals dramatically how far this western world is from that of the eastern shore.

Edna St. Vincent Millay describes how we train lovers feel when she says,

*"My heart is warm with the friends I make.*

*And better friends I'll not be knowing.*

*But there isn't a train I wouldn't take.*

*No matter where it's going."*

In Europe, the T.E.E. (*Transcontinental European Express*) are crack daytime-only trains that are all first class, luxuriously equipped, full restaurant service (some with restaurant cars, others serving meals at every seat) fully air-conditioned, and operating at high speeds.

When we boarded the *Transalpin* in Zurich, Switzerland, what a surprise and delight it was to have a uniformed waiter greet us, presenting us with a luncheon menu and request for reservations. Paul, who spoke five languages, said he hoped we would have a pleasant journey. The trip was ten hours of beautiful mountain scenery of the Tyrol and Austrian Alps through Innsbruck, Salzburg, and Linz to Vienna. Luncheon was served at noon, and our table was resplendent with white tablecloth, silver, napkins, and fresh flowers. The five course meal accompanied by wine and liqueurs was gourmet. All the passengers lingered in the dining car for at least three hours enraptured by the beauty of the scenery. The extras are worth the added fare, we believe. We weren't aware of the high speed even as we sipped our wine since there was little motion.

The *Flying Scot* is another famous train that runs from London to Edinburgh in six hours during the daytime. Two classes are offered, and since we had time, we investigated both. The first class carriages held six passengers and seemed very confining. We opted for the second class car that was open and had tables for every passenger, which were convenient for playing cards, writing letters, or having a meal.

In England, Elderhostel had arranged for private railway cars to take us to the Midlands, Devon, and Cornwall. Had we expected to travel about the country, we would have bought a Britrail Pass before leaving home.

For an extended vacation in Switzerland, we did buy a Swiss Holiday Pass that was valid for as long as thirty days. It is said that no location in Switzerland is more than ten miles from a passenger railway. In fact, this small country is called the turntable of Europe. Its trains are noted for safety and service. Because of this, we elected one August to stay in a small hotel, the Krebs, in Berne across the street from a railway terminal. Every day we crossed to the station, checked the timetable posted and chose our destination for that day. It was a fascinating adventure that took us to Zermatt, Lucerne, Geneva, Neuchâtel, Grindelwald, Thun, and Lausanne. Our Swiss Holiday card assured us half price tickets on both the cable to Mt. Pilatus and the steamer on Lake Geneva. Seeing the Matterhorn and Jungfrau was unforgettable.

The best part of this experience was being able to return each night to the same hotel. We had no luggage to manage as all of our excursions were in the daytime.

Although European trains seem to have plenty of room for bicycles, baggage space is limited. Besides, there are few porters at the railway stations. One must manage his own luggage. Earlier I told a story about arriving in Seville in the rain. If that nice young Spaniard hadn't helped us with our bags, I shudder to think what we would have done.

Of course if you are on a guided tour, arrangements will be made for your luggage. But those who travel independently should carry the minimum wardrobe, preferably in suitcases with wheels.

In Switzerland on the passenger trains, there is one Swiss to two foreigners (business travelers, tourists, and those working for the hotel industry). The profit balance between freight and passenger is one to one. Ours between freight and passenger is twenty to one.

The welcoming phrase on the railroad ticket is *Gute Reise, Bon Voyage,* or *Buon Viaggio* - no Good Day for the Americans!

English is seldom spoken, so at least a smattering of German or French will be a great help, especially to choose an entrée on the menu in a dining car or buffet car. Even when buying something from trolley cars (*vende ambulantes*), it is easier to choose your sandwich, soft drink, or beer if you own a

French or German dictionary. I like a dictionary which gives English into French, as well as French into English.

Pullman reservations vary, depending on whether you go first or second class. An economical solution to overnight sleeping is the couchette, a simple sleeper with blanket, pillow, and small towel provided. In first class the compartment takes four passengers, in second, six.

Our first experience with a couchette was en route from Ostend, Belgium to Berne, Switzerland. We had to walk through four cars filled with young wine-drinking students before reaching our couchette. The ticket agent in Victoria Station had assured us we would be the only occupants, but along with our names on the door was another, M. Gautier, Brussels.

We made ourselves comfortable in the two lower bunks, hoping that M. Gautier wouldn't mind sleeping in an upper. I kept on my dress, but took off my shoes as I stretched out. Soon the motion of the train rocked us to sleep,

We were awakened by a rap on the door. Half asleep, Harry went to open it. He fell back as a lovely young girl stepped into the compartment. *"Bon soir, Madame-M'sieu"*, she said in a lilting voice.

"Where do you like to sleep?" Harry asked, a bit embarrassed.

She pointed to the top berth. *"Ici.* I like thees one. Is all right?"

Relieved we chorused, "Great."

As she began to take off her dress, we hastily climbed into our berths. Would she take off all her clothes? But no, she still had on a slip when she climbed the ladder and slipped out of sight. *"Bonne nuit,"* was the last we heard from her that night. We didn't see her again because our train reached Berne at six in the morning, and she was sound asleep when we left.

Later, our European friends told us always to sleep in an upper, because travelers in lower bunks had been robbed. Although we had slept better than usual in our couchette, it wasn't likely we would take another. Suppose there had been four strangers sharing that compartment with us?

No railway story can be complete without a mention of the *Orient Express,* the elegant train used by the rich and famous in the '20s and '30s. Because of entrepreneur James Sherwood, an Englishman, this splendid train has been restored by master artisans and may be boarded in London, Paris, Zurich, Innsbruck, Salzburg, and Vienna for a day trip or for the full itinerary. It is too expensive for our budget, but we have seen the red carpeted platform and deluxe carriages with their rosewood marquetry and Art Deco.

In Vienna, we met an English couple who had just arrived from Paris on the *Orient Express.* They had been part of a select group and worn special formal attire for the trip. However, they found sleep was impossible because of the old carriages bumping together and were sorry they had spent so much money and had so little comfort.

Other friends loved their trip from Vienna to Munich leaving in the late afternoon, and arriving at 10 p.m. The scenery through the Bavarian Alps was spectacular, and they were looking forward to a pleasant dinner, only to find their dining car had been transferred to another section going on to Paris. You can imagine how hungry they were on arrival in Munich!

The Thomas Cook International Timetable is indispensable for railway travel abroad. It's published monthly in London and imported by Travel Library. Orders can be sent to Travel Library, P.O. Box 249, Department F, La Canada, Calif. 91011.

If you plan to see much of Europe, buying a Eurailpass before you leave home, and at the same time making seating and sleeping reservations will assure you a carefree vacation at a low cost. You will know exactly what your travel will cost; the Eurailpass map and timetable will act as a guide. You will sit in the first class sections of the best trains, and you will have discounts on Europabus trips.

The Southern Railway System has a jingle about train travel:

*An experienced traveler we know,*

*Chooses trains as the best way to go.*

*He gets a lot of rest*

*Arrives feeling his best.*

*With no worries about fog, sleet, or snow.*

# 5

# ADVENTURE BY FREIGHTER

*Freighter, Austral Envoy, Sidney, Australia, 1991.*

# ADVENTURE BY FREIGHTER

"Who would ever want to travel on a freighter?" is a question often asked us whenever we talk about cargoliners.

Usually we launch into why we like these long voyages so much. Had they ever noticed how inexpensive the fare was compared to a large ocean liner's? The four to twelve passengers have outside cabins with private facilities; time is not organized except for meals; all ships are air conditioned, and a few have laundry rooms with washing machines and dryers. There is no doctor, but the first officer attends to minor accidents. Otherwise, an ill person is transferred to a hospital at the nearest port. My enthusiasm shines through as I relate days at sea, relaxing. The ship is our home with the officers and crew, our friends.

My love affair with freighters began in 1939 when a college friend and I decided to take a tramp steamer to Italy. We had earned our fare, so our parents couldn't object, although no one we knew had ever ventured abroad on a cargo ship. Our *Birmania* sailed from New York with ten passengers on board. The brochure said the voyage would last fifty-two days, stopping at Trieste, Fiume, Venice, Naples, and Genoa. The total cost was $270!

How relieved we were to find our Italian Line ship was spotless, and our cabin was spacious with two closets and windows. The Italian officers were attentive to our needs; the captain was delighted to have two young, unmarried ladies aboard. The food was Italian, and at Venice I found my knees were too painful for me to climb the bridges over the canals. An officer, versed in medicine, although not a doctor, said I wasn't used to a spaghetti diet and ordered salads instead. He was right. Then I faced reality; I had gained so much weight, all my clothes were tight. Nevertheless, we realized what a wonderful time we had had, playing deck sports, watching the ever-changing sea, and at night, dancing in the saloon with the young officers.

There was a bad storm sailing though the Atlantic, and the captain let us up on the bridge to watch the waves break over the bow. Luckily neither of us were seasick. I especially remember dropping anchor off Venice and the gondoliers coming out to greet us. Unfortunately, tramp steamers disappeared a long time ago.

Still remembering that experience, I found a book in our library, *Ford's Freighter Travel Guide,* that listed freighters sailing all over the world. A friend gave me a freighter magazine, *Traveltips.* It was difficult to decide on our ship as well as our destination.

Freighters have changed since my tramp steamer days. Now some carry cargo, previously packaged, in large metal containers, and these are piled high on the forward deck. This method enables the ships to unload and reload so fast that often they only need to stay in port one day. There is no longer much space for passengers to promenade. However, some still remain bulk cargo ships.

The *Zvir* was one of these. She sailed from Savannah, Georgia to the Mediterranean, her destination Rijeka, Yugoslavia. We liked the fact there were fifty passengers on the *Zvir.* Even so she had two classes, tourist and first. The only spaces left were in tourist, so we took them. A doctor was on board, and as the ship was not containerized, there would be room for us to move about. The *Zvir* was an old ship but well maintained. Most of the officers spoke little English and the crew none.

There was no news of the outside world, a hardship for the American passengers. Harry asked the chief steward if we could write a newsletter. After consulting with the captain, he said he would be delighted to let us use the typewriter in his cabin. The Yugoslavian keyboard was foreign, but Harry used his hunt and peck system.

A passenger with a short wave radio and I would station ourselves under a lifeboat to pick up the news from BBC and the *Voice Of America.*

Harry typed the daily news, weather reports, and whatever the captain wanted the passengers to know, news of a fire drill, an invitation to his cocktail party, a tour of the engine room, or something about our ports of call.

The passengers received our newsletter so enthusiastically they lined up to see the bulletin outside the dining saloon where it was posted every noon. Both classes had identical bulletins. Our newsletters continued and became increasingly important when we entered the Mediterranean where the captain reported unscheduled stops, the first being in Morocco.

On the *Zvir*, officers and crew were Yugoslavian. As Socialists, seamen were encouraged to mingle with the passengers for the social hour in the bar. They were clean, but wore their work clothes, quite different from the officers in their khaki uniforms. There was not much interchange because they spoke no English; but later, after dinner, they entertained us on deck singing ballads of the Balkans in deep bass voices.

On this freighter there were no washing machines, so wives were busy doing laundry and hanging it out on deck to dry. Only those in tourist did this, as staterooms in first class were large enough for a clothesline.

In Naples, Captain Lally's wife boarded the ship and proceeded to wash his clothes. She traveled with us all the way to Rijeka and looked after him as she would at home. After we left Morocco, there were nights at sea when we all craved entertainment. Our idea to have a masquerade met with little enthusiasm, so we decided to wear costumes and surprise everyone. Cold cream mixed with burnt sienna watercolor (as an artist, I always carried paint) was just right to darken our complexions. I used Payne's gray to give Harry a beard, moustache, and dark eyebrows.

We then draped a sheet about his tall figure to resemble a jellaba and covered his head with a towel held in place by a scarf. When he took off his glasses, Harry really looked like a Berber chief. I wore a long dress I had bought from a vendor in Marrakech and covered my head and the lower part of my face with a thin veil.

As we entered the dining saloon, a hush fell. Then passengers whispered, "When did they get on? Did they come from Agadir?" No one guessed who we were. Finally, when two men offered us their chairs, we broke out laughing, and everyone said, "The Lymans!"

When we entered the officers' quarters, they rose to their feet and bowed, smiling broadly. We couldn't fool them. Plainly delighted with our costumes, they offered us places at their table and poured glasses of wine.

Another evening the chief engineer, Ivan Beloc, invited us to his cabin to show us something. Intrigued, we went to his quarters and found he had made a miniature replica of Columbus' ship, the *Santa Maria*, a beautifully crafted model with many small wooden pieces. The officer startled us with "Mr. and Mrs. Lyman, this ship sailed to America where there is freedom. We too love freedom. My country is poor, yours is rich, but we both love freedom." There were tears in his brown eyes. It was a very moving experience.

This first voyage was a revelation. Life on a freighter has so many attractions and so much time to relax with no one to organize what you do. So many friends have said, "But what do you do with so many days at sea? There isn't much entertainment, is there?" When we told them we were content to read, play an occasional game of scrabble, or bridge, and listen to tapes of classical music, they shook their heads and exclaimed,"No video, or movies?"

After this enjoyable freighter trip, Harry suggested we visit South America. The Ivaran Norwegian Line's *S.S. Salvador* was scheduled to leave Houston the end of August, bound for Buenos Aires and Rio. Brazil required a visa, so we sent for ours before leaving for New England. There was a warning note that we must apply for our visas near to our departure date, but in our case, this wasn't possible. However, after we arrived in Houston and talked to the ship's agent, we began to worry.

Our ship would stop in Brazil on its voyage southward and then return on its northbound trip. There was a question about how long we would be in Argentina and Uraquay. Would our Brazilian visa expire if the stay in Buenos Aires was longer? Our agent suggested we talk to the Brazilian Embassy in Houston. The man there said there would be no problem. We could enter Brazil on our current visa on both southern and northern trips. "Have a good time," he said. "Spend plenty of money!" Reassured, we sailed south stopping to pick up cargo at small cities along the eastern coast of South America.

There was a swimming pool on this freighter, a bonus as the weather was warm. Time flew as the days were broken up by a sandpiper flying on deck and a consultation among the eight passengers about what to feed him, and then a surprising experience.

One day our engines were stopped for repair off the coast of Brazil. Suddenly there was a cry from the bridge. "Whales!" boomed Captain Helge from the bridge. Sure enough, as close as twenty feet from our ship, three whales cavorted, diving under the hull, and around it. We could even see their eyes and teeth. Later the captain explained that the huge mammals had grown curious because our ship was floating silently. They had come to investigate.

We were too busy having a good time to think about our visas. However, on our northbound voyage, the first morning after docking in Santos, Brazil, a travel agent came aboard with plans for sightseeing that day. She read the list of passengers, but our names weren't there. "There's some mistake," I cried. "We want to go ashore and see Santos."

"I was told your visas have expired," she said.

Harry and I gasped. "But the man at the Houston Embassy assured us our visas would be valid for the entire trip," Harry said angrily. I was too upset to speak.

She looked at us sympathetically. "I'm sorry, but I have my orders. You must remain on the ship."

We watched our fellow passengers gather their cameras, passports, and visas, preparatory to leaving the ship. We never felt more alone as they went down the gangplank to the pier and followed the guide to the waiting bus.

"Perhaps we'll only be unloading here a day," Harry said to cheer me.

I pointed to the burlap bags of coffee on the dock. More cargo was arriving, and with sinking heart, I knew our stay would be at least three or four days.

Our stewardess, Christine, was most sympathetic. Fortunately, she spoke Portuguese and offered to call the American Embassy on the ship's phone. However, it was out of order for the entire time we were in port, so there was no way we could reach any American representative there. We were virtually prisoners on the *Salvador*!

That day our ship was silent except for our talking over a half-hearted game of scrabble. We had tossed our notes about Santos and what we had planned to do into a wastebasket. Not able to face our friends when they climbed back on the ship exchanging anecdotes about what they'd seen, we stayed in our cabin.

Although a notice had been posted on the bulletin board near the dining saloon about Captain Helge's cocktail party before dinner, we decided to skip the occasion. This was the first time we couldn't enjoy joining the officers and passengers.

There was a knock on our door. It was Tony, the first officer. Had we forgotten the captain's party? We told him we felt we had nothing to say since we hadn't been allowed to leave the ship. Tony, a gregarious person, was crestfallen. "Without you there's no fun," he said. "Captain Helge asked me to tell you he wants to talk to you about your situation." He persuaded us to return with him to the lounge where everyone greeted us warmly and told us how much they had missed us.

After we had a drink, Captain Helge took us aside. This wasn't the first time he had trouble with Brazilian authorities. Lately, anti-American sentiment had increased.

"Please do not tell anyone, but just go ashore with the others tomorrow morning, only be sure you walk the full length of the dock and go through the far gate. That one is not fully manned, and it's unlikely they will be looking for you there." The captain turned and joined the other passengers.

We felt like drug smugglers as we stepped up to the last gate and hurried through to the busy street beyond. Because we thought that we would never see Santos, the city took on new interest. By taking the cable car to the mountain summit, we had a view of the harbor, our ship, and the city below -

breathtaking. While having lunch near the Botanical Garden, we met an English lady, the widow of a coffee broker, who invited us to her stately home now surrounded by skyscrapers. Her tales of the early days, when life for the English and Americans had been gracious, were interesting.

In addition to more cargo than usual, we had to wait until certain papers arrived to clear portions of the cargo. As a result, our ship remained in Santos a week.

Each day the guard at the far gate let us pass, but near the end of our stay, the captain sent for us. A couple from California had been detained and questioned at length about their visas. The guards were looking for us. The captain cautioned us to stay on board, for fines and imprisonment might result if the authorities arrested us. The ship would have to leave without us!

After that, our only stops were small Brazilian ports, and no one bothered to ask about our visas.

Once home, I wrote the Brazilian Embassy in Houston, but there was no reply or apology for our detention. Our painful experience made us realize how important a visa can be.

By now, freighter voyages seemed the only way to travel. Our next adventure took us to New Zealand and Australia, a trip that would never be forgotten. The countries Down Under were fascinating, but on our way home, we encountered weather and danger that threatened my life.

On this voyage, our ship was the American *Austral Envoy* that left Charleston, S. C., bound for Brisbane, Australia. Freighters never arrive the day expected, but this one was a week late. Sightseeing in Charleston was pleasant, but we grew impatient, wondering if our ship would ever dock.

Finally she appeared, as we waited on the pier. This freighter was unlike the others, seeming derelict with little paint, and a general uncared for look, not a bit like the photo the Line had sent me. Harry was unperturbed, saying she was riding high because she was empty and would be painted after they took on cargo.

Our luggage was tossed with boxes into a net and swung aboard the ship. Even the gangway with its steep ascent and slippery lines filled me with foreboding.

At the Panama Canal, the bo'sun told us the *Austral Envoy* was the longest freighter to pass through that day (813.17 ft.) The year before she had been stretched amidships to make more room for cargo and refrigerated space. "She's weak in the middle now, and the captain's got to be very careful how he handles her in rough weather," he said.

Imagine our relief to find smooth sailing across the Pacific, and, even on our return, only a few thunderstorms interrupted sunny weather. Then, as we began to pack preparatory to arriving in Philadelphia, the line storm hit just north of Cape Hatteras.

Our jokes about the chairs and tables anchored to the deck were suddenly not funny.

Captain Stanejko gave orders for all possessions to be locked in bureaus and closets. No one was to walk on deck, but to sit in the lounge. From there, we watched our ship sink into deep troughs of foamy sea, and then rise so high all we could see was gray sky.

Everything aboard, that was not battened down, shifted back and forth with each shudder of the vessel. All the books from our passengers' library mingled with jars of peanut butter from the snack bar.

Laura, a widow from New Orleans, started to cross the lounge when a sudden lurch sent her flying against the bulkhead. Two of the men managed to help her to a chair, but she was in great pain. Later, we found her arm had been broken.

There were only a few of us at dinner. Right afterward we retired to our cabin. Harry slept in a regular size bed, but mine was a Murphy sofa that converted at night into my bed. Two pins were used to keep it in place but early on, we noticed only one pin was holding the bed down and asked our steward to replace the missing one. He had not done so.

Worn out by the shaking and shuddering of our ship, and too worried to read, we turned off our lights and finally went to sleep. In the middle of the night, the ship shook so that I awoke. Then I heard Harry cry out. I snapped on my light and saw him carried across the cabin on his mattress as if it were a flying carpet. Finally he landed with a thump and let out a howl.

"Are you all right?" I asked. He responded with a groan. "I've banged my right toe." He went back to sleep on his mattress that lay on the floor.

Later on there was a terrible crash. Had our ship snapped in two? Half awake, I found my bed rising. My pin had slipped out, and I was going up into the wall. Just as the bed was about to close, I stuck my finger in the crack in order to have air to breathe. I've always had a fear of suffocating.

I then called Harry, but from where I lay at the base of the sofa, my voice couldn't project enough for him to hear me. After many attempts to wake him, I grew desperate. Then when I had almost given up, I heard him say, "June, where are you?" What a relief! Then he yelled, "My God, the bed's closed!" and heard him open the door and call Jim in the next cabin.

I tried to keep calm, recalling an old Lucy Ball movie when she had disappeared into the wall just as I had. I even giggled.

Jim arrived, and he and Harry began to tug at the bed, but to no avail. My weight acted as a fulcrum. "She's got to climb out," Jim said. "I'll go get some of the crew."

"But she's only wearing a short nightgown," Harry cried.

"Your wife's life is at stake, and you're worrying about someone seeing her undressed!" Jim sounded disgusted.

"Get a glass of water, will you?" Harry said. Considering his state of mind, I though he was being very considerate. The excitement had made my mouth dry.

I was beginning to ache crammed into such a small space. I managed to shift positions and raise myself a little, wondering how I would ever climb up over the side.

After what seemed a very long time, the men returned.

Jon, the first officer, had come and with him the bo'sun and steward. Jon took charge. "We'll have to grab hold of her arms."

"Take it easy," Harry said. "She's not very strong, and besides, she doesn't have much on."

"Why don't you sit down and let us handle this," Jon suggested.

"Thanks for the water. I really needed it," Harry said. And I thought he was thinking of me!

Then I felt them tug at the bed. "Mrs. Lyman, can you give me your hands?" came Jon's voice. They had opened the crack enough to allow their arms inside and I reached up and grabbed hold. Gradually I was able to almost stand up. "Hook your leg over the side," Jon directed. Luckily I had kept in shape doing daily aerobics. I lifted a leg over the edge as they supported my arms. Harry reached in to pull down my nightgown. With one final heave, I perched on the side and brought my other leg over. Jumping down into outstretched arms, I never thought how I must have looked. Was I ever glad to be free again!

Harry covered me with a blanket, and hugged me so hard I lost my breath. When everyone had gone, he squeezed me again and said, "Those guys were perfect gentlemen. Nobody looked at you."

"Not very flattering," I said with a laugh. "You know, if I'd dreamed this would be happening to me, I would have worn pajamas."

When we returned home, our friends were more interested in hearing about the storm and how I was trapped in a sofa bed than our adventures in New Zealand.

Our freighter experiences were often as unexpected as the above. Sometimes we were disappointed, such as when we were unable to see important cities like Rio because of a long wait for a berth in the harbor. When we did sail into port, it was dark and too late to go ashore. The next morning we sailed away having a wonderful view of Sugar Loaf, but never setting a foot in the city. Famous places like Iguassu Falls were out of the question, since reservations must be made weeks in advance, and our ship was never sure of its schedule.

However, there were many unexpected visits arranged by the Line. One was to Ciritiba, the capital of Parana, and the other to a Heidleburg type city, Blumenau. These extras were compliments of the Ivaran Line.

On our Yugoslavian trip, the government hosted us for a week in Rijeka, the Yugolinja Line's headquarters. There we stayed in a lovely hotel situated on the Adriatic and were given tours of the surrounding country to promote travel in Yugoslavia.

In New Zealand, our ship changed its schedule and only made a day's stop at Auckland. How lucky we were that we'd decided to fly over from Australia and spend two weeks in New Zealand while our ship picked up cargo at various Australian ports.

There are three A's of freighter travel. You must

be *"Able"* - there is no doctor or tourbus to meet you when your ship arrives, *"Adjustable"* because nothing is certain - the date you leave, the ports of call, or the congeniality of the few passengers. We were lucky to meet some nice people, but there is always one person who is not agreeable. Seasoned travelers do not let anyone spoil their voyage. The third A of freighter travel is a passenger should be *"Adventurous."* Exploring seldom called-on ports can be very exciting when you leave the ship on your own.

I have tried to give a true picture of freighter travel. It is not for everyone, but if you love the sea and like to be on it for any length of time, if you have the inner resources to be happy with simple pleasures, and if you like to talk with people of all nationalities and walks of life, freighters are the way to go. Each ship has its own personality. The same may be true of the officers and crew of various countries.

Compared with luxury cruises, this way of travel is economical. The service and food are good, and accommodations compare favorably. All cabins command good views. Reservations should be made a year in advance with the clause, "to be ready on a day's notice", often inserted.

Here's a word about clothes for a freighter. Wash and wear slacks and tops are the rule for women with two or three dresses or suits for evening wear. Most people like to change their clothes for dinner, and although men need not wear jackets and ties, for special occasions they do. Dining ashore in hotels calls for jackets and ties for men. Formal clothes are never worn, so they can be left at home. Be sure to include bathing suits as many of the new cargoliners have swimming pools.

The best way to decide on which voyage appeals to you is to subscribe to *Traveltips*, a bimonthly magazine. There are Freighter Cruise Listings as well as Traveltips Exclusive Trips that offer members voyages at special rates. Every month there are new Freighter Lines listed, and also new ships such as Ivaran's *Americana* that has deluxe accommodations for 88 passengers. Of interest too, are the personal accounts of passengers. Details of various voyages are described and may influence your choice of Line and destination.

Harry and I found our freighter trips to be most enjoyable.

# 6

# TO TRAVEL AND TO LEARN (THE ELDERHOSTEL WAY)

*Elderhostel, Red Fox Alpine Inn, Jeffersonville, Vermont, 1989.*

# TO TRAVEL AND TO LEARN
## (THE ELDERHOSTEL WAY)

Marty Knowlton, an American educator, devised an ingenious plan inspired by the folkhighschools in Scandinavia and the youth hostels in Europe designed to enrich the lives of people past school age. To live together and learn at the same time appealed to Mr. Knowlton, and with this idea he approached colleges and universities. His students would be over sixty and able to live in the dormitories when colleges weren't in session. Professors, too, could be used for this program of continuing adult education.

Accommodations would be modest and the food simple in order to attract people of all walks of life and varying degrees of education. And so *Elderhostel* was born and has been growing fast ever since its beginning.

In 1989, over 190,000 hostelers enrolled in these programs in all fifty states, all Canadian provinces, and forty countries overseas.

Most programs last one week, beginning on Sunday afternoon and ending Saturday morning. Three courses are offered every day, each lasting an hour and a half. Only one course is required, but you can attend all three if you choose.

You live simply in dormitory rooms furnished with twin beds and eat wholesome, but plain food in the cafeterias. Now, the program has grown so much, some facilities are in conference centers, summer camps, retreats, and national park lodges.

How does travel enter into *Elderhostel*? One must go from his or her home to the college selected. Usually hostelers prefer to explore another state or part of the country. A car, train, or bus is taken with the expense underwritten by the hosteler. Once you are registered, the staff will let you know travel alternatives. Our program cost $275 which included registration, six nights' accommodations, all meals, five days of classes, and a variety of extra-curricular activities.

The International Program involves more time and money, because the price includes international round-trip airfare and all travel and transfers within the country, full room and board, complete academic instruction, excursions and admission fees, various evening performances, and limited accident, sickness, and baggage insurance. Programs abroad last three or four weeks.

*Elderhostels* don't appeal to everyone. Some find the idea of sharing a bath unthinkable, and as for eating in a cafeteria, forget it! But if you can do without luxuries, you'll appreciate the intellectual smorgasbord that's being offered.

Harry and I have attended ten *Elderhostels* in the U.S. and two abroad, in Scandinavia at folkhighschools, and in England at colleges. One of the most memorable was in Scandinavia.

In Sogndal, our folkhighschool (folkehogskule) overlooked the Sogne Fjord. There were thirty of us hostelers, and all were eager to know more about the culture and history of Norway.

That morning after breakfast, our class met. Kari Thorsen, our young blonde teacher, suggested we start every morning by singing a Norwegian song. She sat down at the piano and played the piece, after which we tried to hum the melody.

Thus began a memorable stay in which we manned an ancient Norse sailing ship, the exact replica of the famous Gokstad. It resembled an old galley, and under the direction of Nels, we hoisted the battered sail and rowed across the fjord.

We visited a typical farm that had produced fruit and vegetables for six generations. Its owner,

Knute Hagvar, was proud of his twenty acres, and of the fact that he didn't have to import anything as he grew barley and grain. During his short growing season, his four children helped with picking fruit and feeding cattle.

Another visit was to a manor house near the folkhighschool. Wibeke Knagenhjelm, a lumber baron, welcomed our group. While his wife offered us tea, he told about the manor being occupied by the Nazis during World War II. An imposing residence, it overlooked the fjord and piles of lumber waiting for shipment. His company supplies the Norwegian government with most of its lumber to make fences and telephone poles.

An unexpected invitation came from a famous artist who lived in Fronningan on an island reached by boat. Knut Rumohr, a Norwegian painter known for his modern paintings, showed his private collection of old buildings and his gallery. Some of us bought small landscapes to bring home.

These three visits were in addition to our daily classes, in which we learned about Norwegian history, music, agriculture, education, and geology. This latter was explained further by a trip to the Nigard Glacier noted for its blue ice.

Since many of our lives had been touched by Hitler, it was interesting to learn that four thousand Norwegians had died and that half of their navy had been lost. After the war trials had been held for collaborators, thirty had been executed.

On one bus excursion, we saw the remains of a bridge, blown up by the Norwegians before the Nazis came and what was left of a town destroyed by the Germans in retaliation.

In one week, we all felt a part of Norway because of the young instructors eager to tell us about their country and its culture. When we went by ferry from Kaupanger Hovedgard to Stavkyrkje, the music of Edvard Greig accompanied us as our boat followed the deep fjord through the mountains.

Our accommodations were in a simple lodge, our rooms bare, but clean. The meals were carrots, boiled potatoes, and smoked fish; sometimes onions were added. This was our only complaint, the same menu every night. But the last night, we had salmon. However, this was a poor school, and their budget was slim.

In contrast, when we arrived in Denmark, the Norgarde Hojskole was in a lovely flower garden with handsome modern buildings. We had traveled by bus to Oslo and taken the overnight ferry to Fredrolsjavn in Denmark. The drive through Jutland's rolling farmlands was beautiful. Here Grundvig started the folkhighschool to raise the education level and enrich the lives of the farmers.

There was a large enclosed swimming pool and a craft room that had twenty looms for weaving. The picturesque town of Berringbro was within walking distance of the school.

There was an exchange of local people with the hostelers. This involved a dinner invitation to a nearby farm where two or three of us could become acquainted with our hosts and their lives in Denmark. Ours was a young couple who lived some distance away on a farm where they raised a special breed of horses. The girl had a wealthy mother who didn't approve of their living together without benefit of marriage. Theirs was an old farmhouse with the kitchen on the first floor and living-dining room with adjacent bedroom on the second floor. Our dinner was delicious, still warm although carried from the kitchen below. The silver and bone china seemed elegant after the plain fare at Elderhostel.

Our young host spoke fluent English and often interpreted for his girl. They showed us their stables and the horses that had won so many awards in international competition. The following evening our Danish friends had dinner at our folkhighschool, and enjoyed our sing-a-long.

Our last week in Scandinavia we went by bus to Fredrikshavn where a ferry took us to Gothenburg, Sweden. Our Folkhogskola, a part of the Lutheran

Church, was in ancient town of Sigtuna, overlooking Lake Malaren.

Our accommodations were the best we'd had with private bath, and the dining room and lounge were decorated with murals. Our sleeping quarters were on a hill above the classroom area, and required a walk up a steep hill, a hardship for some of the older Elderhostelers. There was a ballroom where one evening a local folk dance troop put on an exhibition in which we joined. Our courses were on Sweden, its economy, history, geography, and culture. Its policy of neutrality interested us.

The town of Sigtuna has an eleventh century church and other historical monuments. It reminded us of Williamsburg. Bus excursions took us to the palace of Venngarn that is now used as a sanitarium for alcoholics. An artist on the premises opened his studio for us and demonstrated his method of painting. Being on hand to see another artist painting a hunting scene in a new church was of interest to us all.

Another excursion was by boat to the seventeenth century palace of Skokloster which still has its original, rich furnishings.

This Elderhostel was different from the others because it was run by a minister of the Lutheran Church who owned the folkhighschool. The classes were regimented with little humor. Meals were good and well served. Here we were strictly on our own as far as carrying luggage, but the male hostelers helped anyone in difficulty on the steep paths.

One evening was designated as "Meet the Swede" night. We were assigned to a family that consisted of a taxi driver, his wife who spoke no English, and their ten year old daughter eager to use her limited English. I think the father volunteered to join the program because of his little girl. Unlike Denmark, this was anything but a tranquil experience. The small house was very untidy, a small dog kept jumping on us, and the dinner was partially burned.

The next evening, when the father and daughter came as our guests, the situation changed. The mother remained at home, and everyone seemed anxious to have a good time. After dinner, the hostelers entertained the Swedish guests with humorous skits. Harry and I sang an old barbershop song, *She's More To Be Pitied Than Censored.* To dramatize my plight, I stuffed a pillow under my dress to appear pregnant and wore a sunhat pulled over my eyes. When we sang,

*Do not laugh at her shame and downfall.*

*For a moment just stop and consider,*

*that a man was the cause of it all!*

I drooped dejectedly, and Harry folded his arms, the supreme male. To our surprise, the Swedish guests roared with laughter, and as did our hosteler friends who later asked if we'd been rehearsing our performance.

You don't have to go abroad to enjoy the Elderhostel experience. There are programs offered in every state. What a choice there is, too! The theater, computer workshops, entomology, painting, art appreciation, gold mining and geology, the brain, parting the Iron Curtain, basic tennis, religion, finding your ancestors - the list goes on and on. Choosing a campus that appeals to you with subjects you want to study should take priority.

We wanted to see other parts of our own country, so we chose various locations, the first being on a small college in West Virginia. It appeared at first like the description in the catalog, beautiful with spacious lawns and ancient elms, but when we entered the women's dormitory where our room was located, we were appalled at the graffiti on the walls and at the lack of maintenance.

No one was there to greet us. Finally, a harassed man hurried up. He was the school's English professor and in charge of the new Elderhostel program. He showed us our room, very small but clean, and supplied us with a pillow and sheets.

Our classes began the next day: Appalachian Folk Culture, Entomology (study of insects), and Mountain Music.

The three instructors made us feel at ease. Until now, we had only wanted to exterminate bugs, but when we looked at ants under a microscope, and then went outside to watch a colony make its way up a hill to a spoon loaded with peanut butter, we were fascinated. A black ant stationed himself near the bait and devoured the smaller ants as they came up. We saw caterpillars emerging from their cocoons, and our favorite after dinner pastime was searching for lunar moths.

One evening to further our understanding of Appalachian culture, our group of twenty-five was driven by a bus to nearby Beckley where, in an amphitheater, there was a play, "Honey in the Rocks" about the civil war and the role West Virginia played. Another treat was a square dance held on the terrace. A keg of beer was provided, and three mountain men played fiddles and a dulcimer, an instrument we had been studying. All of us enjoyed dancing to the lively music. The last night the college president invited us to his gracious home for dessert and coffee.

In 1989, we chose a program, "Outward Bound", at Thompson Island in Boston Harbor. A boat transported us to this island, a privately owned education center where for years a boys' school had been maintained. Now children from Boston's inner city come to study and play five days a week during the summer months. "Outward Bound" to us meant mountain climbing in Colorado. Others may have thought so too because instead of forty hostelers, only eighteen came.

Our apprehension left when we found only the young boys there were expected to climb trees and fences. Our assignment was tame, but in a way, a challenge. Each person slipped a bicycle tire over his or her arm, then joined hands. The object was to pass the tire around the circle without letting go of hands. It was a feat to slip your head and body through the tire and step out of it. One lady, crippled with arthritis, couldn't get the tire over her head. At first, we thought there was no solution, but one smart man pulled us all to her side and helped without letting go of hands. As long as we moved together, we could assist anyone who needed help.

Another problem was for us to take six sticks and form a parallelogram and three triangles. We almost gave up, but one person set the sticks upright to form a tent. It worked! Most of us had only thought about laying the sticks flat on the ground.

An interesting course was one led by Bill Perkins, a naturalist. Every day Bill brought us into the fields, where sometimes the sumac was taller than we were, explaining about wild plants and how we could survive by eating some of them. In contrast, the theater came to life when an English Shakespearean actor currently performing in Boston gave us real insight into the roles of the director, playwright, and actor.

The last course found us under the guidance of an Audubon expert searching for birds in the early morning or evening.

Often our paths crossed those of the young boys from Boston. We could hear them cheering when playing games and singing in the dining room. Once they were given a lesson on how to set the table, and what to do when there is a salad bar. We became acquainted with one of their leaders, a college-educated black man, who had given up his previous career to help boys like these.

That same summer we drove up to Smuggler's Notch, Vermont to attend an Elderhostel program at the Red Fox Alpine Ski Lodge at the foot of Mt. Mansfield. There we ate, slept, and took instruction in the same rustic building. Our professor, head of religion at the University of Vermont, intrigued us the first day with his question. "Who is God?" No one missed a session of this class.

A local artist led an art appreciation and painting class, demonstrating technique in creating a landscape from where we sat high on the mountainside. After the first day, she lost her audience as most of us were so inspired by the beauty around us, we were eager to paint ourselves.

The owner of the ski lodge had lived in the area for many years, so he was well qualified to tell us about the history of Mt. Mansfield. He led a motor caravan around the base of the mountain where even in summer, rocks often block the road. From below, we spotted rare Peregrine falcons and explored tunnels through the massive boulders. Then we drove to the summit where there's a magnificent view and rocky paths to follow along the ridge.

One of the classes Harry and I enjoyed the most was the musical workshop with Fred Waring. It was just before his death and it was held at Pennsylvania State University under an Elderhostel program. Ninety-four of us participated and learned from this master arranger of music. Harry, a barbershopper, had eagerly looked forward to this week on the State College campus. Not a singer, I was glad of a change away from home and chance to learn more about music.

Few of these Elderhostelers had ever sung in any group, yet there were many fine voices. The first morning the instructor, Dr. John Raymond, prevented me from slipping out while the voices were being tested. "We must hear everyone. Let's hear you sing the scale." I complied, thinking that one sound of my low voice would make him realize I was a monotone. To my astonishment, he said, "You're an alto."

Harry was as surprised as I was to find I was in the chorus. It wasn't long before we began an intensive course of forty-five hours of rehearsal and instruction in music philosophy. The success of Fred Waring and his Glee Club has been reported to come from his interest in word enunciation. Mr. Waring's method impressed us with how important it is to sing clearly.

Neither of us had any idea of the scope of our musical training at Penn. State. There would be a performance the last night during which our group would sing thirteen songs. Some were favorites: *Side by Side, This Little Light of Mine, Look for the Silver Lining*. Others were unfamiliar, including the *Opening Number,* my favorite. When we marched into the Eisenhower Auditorium for our big show, all of us were excited and nervous, too, because Mr. and Mrs. Waring and the Waring Blenders were in the audience, as well as the young singers who were studying under Mr. Waring. We had listened to their rehearsals and knew how exacting he could be.

I was assigned to the third row on the risers. As we finished our first song, we were to throw up our arms and say, "This is the end of our opening number!" This was my first time on any stage, so I gave it all I had. When the end came, I threw up my arms with such force, I lost my balance and fell over backward, sitting down on the feet of a singer standing on the riser behind me. She let out a groan as I fell from sight. I lay there, thankful that the audience and especially the Warings in the first row couldn't see what happened to me. Harry, luckily, was in front of me.

I managed to stand up for the next number, certain that no one had seen me fall, but when we marched out at the close of the show, two girls came up. "What happened to you? You just disappeared."

I explained I had lost my balance. "I guess I was carried away by being in the limelight," I said.

"Aren't you glad you weren't on the top riser?" one girl said. We all agreed I'd been lucky.

As we continue to sing, we think of Fred Waring and that musical learning experience we had during our Elderhostel week at Penn. State. I now leave singing from a riser to Harry!

Some of the Elderhostel courses are very popular. A year ago we signed up for a watercolor workshop in Maine and found we were forty-fifth on the waiting list! It pays to send in your choices as soon as possible to avoid disappointments. Six catalogs are mailed out during the year. Copies may be found in the public library.

Remember, Elderhostels are meant to enrich your

life. No competition is involved, for there are no grades, and no credits are given. Originally, it was supposed to appeal to someone with little education, but the reverse is true. Many PhD's and graduate students are found in the classes.

College professors were lukewarm about the program at first, but now realize how enthusiastic and knowledgeable their Elderhostel students are. They present a challenge that educators welcome. No one is aware of age. The emphasis is on an inquisitive mind and searching for new experiences. Whoever becomes an Elderhosteler will find new friends, new spheres of influence, and a widened horizon.

# 7

# INDEPENDENT TRAVEL

*Crossing on the ferry to Victoria, B. C., 1982.*

# INDEPENDENT TRAVEL

Traveling on your own can be an adventure, but careful planning must be done in advance in order to enjoy your trip. Using such complete guides as Fodor's *Europe*, it is easy to find accommodations to suite your budget, the transportation available, the time best suited for a visit considering the weather, and the number of people apt to be there.

For individual travelers, a reliable travel agent can plan itineraries with an eye to special airfare reductions and hotel reservations. Even though there may be a fifteen percent service charge, your agent will save you time, money, and aggravation if tickets and hotel rooms are reserved before you leave home.

There are some tourists who resist traveling in a group, but prefer to be independent, planning their own trips according to their budgets, tastes, and state of health. For them, meeting a deadline to board the bus each morning and arriving at a destination exhausted is unthinkable. The packing and unpacking that's required when stops are only overnight can be tiresome, too.

One answer for these independent travelers is Grand Circle Travel's Extended Vacation Plan. Grand Circle is a large company that specialize in serving the needs of mature American travelers.

Some prefer a Live Abroad Vacation. Grand Circle pioneered the plan for Americans to live abroad in an apartment or hotel for anywhere from one to twenty-five weeks. There is a Grand Circle Representative on the site to give you tips for exploring on your own. Grand Circle offers this program in Guadalajara, Oaxaca, and London.

More popular is the Extended Vacation Plan. This concept includes spending two weeks or longer in various destinations: Yugoslavia, Mexico, Spain's Costa del Sol, Portugal, Austria, England, or the Swiss Alps. You can combine two destinations or have a Breakaway on your own, but still take advantage of the low cost round trip airfare.

Our first experience with an extended vacation included an economy flight to Lisbon, Portugal where we spent a few days, then on to a charming seaport town, Cascais. The Hotel Cidadela would be our home for a week. After an American type breakfast, the Grand Circle Representative would greet us and sell us tickets to optional excursions to historical landmarks. If we decided to take one, a bus would call at the hotel and take us to surrounding towns. Visits to the Royal Palace at Queluz, the medieval walled city of Obidos, and the fishing village of Navaré gave us insight into Portuguese life.

Days when we chose to remain in the hotel proved relaxing. By exploring side streets in Cascais, we found interesting cafés where we ate lunch. Since we paid for our lunches and dinners, we were free to go wherever we chose.

Some local customs were interesting. In the early morning, fishermen returned from a night of commercial fishing, and as soon as the catch was sorted in a shed near the beach, the natives would crowd in to sit on benches overlooking the fish bins and wait for the auctioneer to begin the bidding, often as lively as any at Sotheby's. The only discordant note in this picturesque town was the drone of mopeds that were cheap enough for most of the young people to own.

Our Grand Circle Representative recommended good restaurants in the area, designating the expensive and moderately priced ones. Dining in a different place every night was an adventure. A local seafood restaurant, the Pescador, was popular.

There were twenty in our Grand Circle group from ten different states. Some sought company; others did not. It was easy to be independent since the only meal we shared was breakfast.

Some of us often chose to dine in our hotel because of entertainment provided by a local troupe specializing in folk dancing.

Grand Circle arranged for us to travel south by bus to our next destination, the Delphim Hotel in the Algarve, an area that stretched along the Mediterranean. Our trip took us through groves of olive and orange trees, across rivers and through mountains that act as a barrier and make the Algarve remote.

The Delphim was a high rise hotel in sharp contrast with the Cicadela with its old world charm and gardens. Instead of lush foliage, there were bare hills that sloped to the Mediterranean. The shoreline and rocky outcroppings were a challenge to any of us who wished to explore. We found these labyrinths difficult to follow and the climbing strenuous.

More appealing were the small restaurants near the sea with their delicious fare of broiled herring washed down with Mateus Rosé. When we weren't exploring, we took a trip to Sagres, where Henry the Navigator planned the sea routes to Africa. Our third week of Grand Circle extended vacation was spent in Madeira off the coast of Africa which is about a four hour flight from Lisbon. Because of its climate, this small island is truly a botanical wonder with flowers and plants of all kinds. As there isn't a level place on the island, the steep mountain slopes are terraced with vineyards. No land is left uncultivated from fruit orchards to vast parks with rare plants. No wonder it is called the "Pearl of the Atlantic."

After Napoleon was defeated at Waterloo, war veterans from Portugal, England and Spain were given parcels of land here. Using contour farming, they developed a productive, as well as beautiful, island.

We stayed at the Sheraton, an "upside-down" hotel. The lobby is on the top floor, the rest of the hotel hugs a steep cliff overlooking the sea. There are swimming pools at three levels. Dining on the terrace overlooking the capital city of Funchal was breathtaking.

Optional tours were offered as in Portugal. As the entire island is rural, these trips involved visiting a wicker furniture factory, stopping by the roadside to watch women and children embroidering blouses, and then later buying the blouses at markets. The Grand Circle Representative recommended trips to Camara de Lobos, the fishing village where Winston Churchill used to paint. At

Santana, we saw a settlement of cottages with thatched roofs.

When we returned home from Portugal and Madeira, we were relaxed and rested. Harry and I felt close to the Portuguese people and their way of life. There is not time to capture this same rapport on a brief tour of the country.

A different kind of Extended Vacation Plan was offered in Spain. In Torremolinos on the Costa del Sol, our accommodations were in a beachfront hotel, the Bajondillo, where our one-bedroom apartment and balcony overlooked the Mediterranean.

The Bajondillo is a way of life for some Americans who return year after year. So many activities are offered: Spanish lessons, aerobics, bridge, handicraft, and dancing every evening under the direction of an international hostess, Doreen Chown. A highlight was a performance by the Malaga ballet troup dancing the flamenco. We studied Spanish, learned how to manipulate the castanets, and listened to a classical guitarist every afternoon.

A Grand Circle representative was at her desk every morning signing us up for excursions to Gibraltar, Malaga, Mijas, Ronda, and Grenada. The latter was our favorite because of the Alhambra Palace.

Another memorable Extended Vacation was in Baden Bei Wein, Austria. Our balcony in the Park

Hotel overlooked a park in which band concerts were given every afternoon. A small opera house stood nearby and, to our delight, light opera was offered during the summer months. One night the theater's ceiling was rolled back to reveal the starlit sky!

The setting of the mountainous Vienna Woods and the picturesque village where only pedestrians could explore became etched in our memories because of its history. During the Soviet occupation after World War II, Mongolian troops were sent into Baden. Fearing for their lives, women and children fled up into Vienna Woods where they hid in caves. Finally, order was restored, and they returned to their homes, but the natives' dislike for Russians is still evident.

In spite of this, Russian officers still vacation in Baden. The top floor of our hotel was reserved for them during our stay. The concert every noon in the town square often included songs like the *Volga Boatman*.

Some of our groups went to Budapest, but in 1984 it was a melancholy city with little to buy. The barbed wire and guards patrolling the Hungarian border depressed us all.

Our Grand Circle representative, Laura, showed us where to catch the bus or train for Vienna an hour away. Sightseeing in the daytime proved enjoyable, returning to Baden in time for dinner. Some opera lovers chose to remain for the evening performances, but it was so late when they returned, we decided to forego that.

As a spa resort, Baden is known for its mineral baths. The charm of the town permeates the attractive shops and restaurants, and there were days when we were content to wander about watching the people and eating in various cafés. The Casino facing the park (Kurpark) was our favorite.

Laura told us of the various daily excursions offered. The bus terminal was the Green Market in the middle of town within easy walking distance. We visited Mayerling (a day's trip) and saw the Memorial Chapel dedicated to the memory of Crown Prince Rudolph. The Benedictine Monastery at Melk impressed us with its fine Baroque architecture, but our plan that day to take a steamer up the Danube proved disappointing. It rained so hard we could scarcely see the water!

Grand Circle came to our assistance in an important way. Needing funds to travel back to London, Harry sent a telex cable to our bank in Boston, but received no answer. Hearing of our difficulty, Laura offered to cash our check for a thousand dollars, no questions asked.

Ours was a congenial group composed mostly of Californians in their sixties. Some of us enjoyed the Olympic size indoor pool in our hotel.

Returning to New York, a Grand Circle representative was waiting to help with ticketing, luggage, and boarding our plane for home.

Grand Circle Travel has been active for twenty-eight years. Because travel agencies and books do not mention it, many travelers are not aware of its existence. To put your name of the mailing list, call their toll free number 1-800-221-2610. Sometimes the lines are busy, and you must wait, but your patience will be rewarded by talking to a courteous Travel Counselor.

The Extended Vacation Plan is a unique way to travel. Besides being able to unpack and stay in one place for a week or longer, you'll have a chance to really know a country and its people.

These countries offer Extended Vacations: Mexico, Bermuda, China, England, Austria, Yugoslavia, Italy, Russia, Spain, Canary Islands, Tahiti, Bora Bora, Australia, Fiji. In addition, you may stay in Hawaii and Florida.

There is a new program called Breakaway in which you can travel on your own after an extended vacation, and still return at a later date using the same low round trip airfare.

Besides being economical, there are bonuses like special cocktail parties, no-fee traveler's checks, an advancement of medical costs in the event you are ill while traveling, $100,000 free travel insurance, visa arrangements, free flight bags, mail delivery at your hotel, and Travel Club discounts. The representatives are fluent in the language of the country you are visiting, and will help with changing currency. For more information, write Grand Circle Travel, 347 Congress Street, Boston, MA 02210 or call 1-800-2610.

Originally it was established to serve the travel needs of the American Association of Retired Persons (AARP). From our experiences, we have found their representatives efficient and friendly and they kept promises to give us affordable and enjoyable vacations.

I haven't mentioned escorted tours and cruises under Grand Circle because this chapter deals with independent travel.

Different from a Grand Circle vacation, but with the same choice of freedom to pursue one's own leisure is a week or more spent at Club Med.

Founded in 1950, this bright new concept of vacationing has grown, and Club Meds have sprung up around the world. Once thought to be for singles and romantic young couples, they now appeal to every age.

Most people have heard of the G.O.'s (*gentil organisateurs*) or congenial hosts who have furthered this dream of quality vacations while offering freedom of choice for the young and young-at-heart.

My bachelor cousin, John, had urged us to vacation at one of the Club Med resorts. He enjoyed the ones in Tahiti and St. Lucia and explained that these clubs had been formed for prisoners of war after World War II, but soon became popular with young people as they were economical, and included a wide variety of sports instruction in their programs. John had learned how to sail and scuba dive and was most enthusiastic.

We made plans to stay at the new Club Med, Buccaneer's Creek, in Martinique. What attracted us at first was the unusual architecture. Buildings in geometric shapes were painted pink, yellow, and blue and seemed to fit the exotic background of plants and the colorful costumes of the natives.

After we signed in, we bought a string of beads to be used to pay for any drink we might want that night. No money would be used at the club. This was especially refreshing since there was no need to carry our wallets to buy cocktails

Our first luncheon delighted us because the outside dining area was in a garden with a barbecue pit for roasting swordfish and snapper caught just that morning. A long buffet table offered many native fruits, pineapple, guavas, avocados, mangos, bananas, and fresh coconut. The fish was served on banana leaves, accompanied by native wine.

It was a feast comparable to any served on a luxury cruise ship. It was hard to leave our wicker chairs to get ready for our sailing lesson. John said the first few days we would sample everything, but later only eat our favorites!

A small fleet of sailboats were anchored in a cove where swashbuckling pirates had hidden while waiting for another ship to plunder. Two young girls and we were the crew with a French instructor barking out orders as we sailed across the bay. We practiced "coming about" until our *derrieres* were sore, but after that first lesson, our confidence grew and sailing became our favorite sport.

We hadn't realized that this was the opening of Buccaneer's Creek, and to celebrate, *Air France* had flown over people from a village. French atmosphere prevailed here. The Congenial Hosts made us feel at home and interpreted for us when they could. We wished we had their fluency in French that first dinner. We were the only Americans and although we knew a little school French, we couldn't keep up with their rapid fire conversation. After a few smiling exchanges, they talked among themselves, and we were left alone.

However, when our daily schedule of sports began, language was forgotten. Gestures with arms and body was enough to teach us sailing and scuba diving.

This first daily contact with the French gave us an insight into their discipline. There were no bulging waistlines or flabby muscles here. Everyone took sports seriously and maintained a good balance of diet and drinking.

The best feature was our freedom to choose what we wanted to do or if we wanted just to rest, no one commented. John had told us that Club Med stressed peace of mind. At five every afternoon, we gathered on the long pier to listen to Chopin and Schumann while assuming a relaxed yoga position. No one was allowed to spoil the quiet by playing a transistor.

A highlight was an afternoon sail to a neighboring island. The yacht had belonged to the Vanderbilts and was a two masted schooner. The French sang lustily and were delighted when we offered *Frere Jacques*.

A barbecue pit had already been dug on the island and red coals were waiting for the fish. The wine didn't seem to affect anyone but us. I even had difficulty peeling the hard boiled eggs, a job assigned to the women guests.

On the way back our sailing instructor pulled me to my feet and began to dance. We whirled about until I had to stop for want of breath.

After dinner every night, the G.O.'s were masters of ceremonies and introduced native girls in colorful costumes who danced a la Martinique. Later, male guests joined them and tried to keep up the calypso beat.

Club Med has changed since we vacationed at Buccaneer's Creek in 1970, but basically it remains the same for it still offers a wide variety of sports concentrating on sailing, snorkeling, aerobics, water exercises, and tennis. Most of the professional instruction still is free, but should you choose horseback riding, golf, or enroll in an arts and crafts program where extra materials are needed, there is an additional charge.

Now the village complexes can be found in thirty-two different countries, and offer an unique opportunity for the entire family. There are over a hundred of them.

Five resorts cater especially to children and grandchildren, allowing the parents and grandparents to enjoy themselves while knowing their offspring are nearby, having fun, too.

The Club Meds are outstanding in four fields. All the clubs emphasize sports and give lessons for improvement. They have circus workshops where one can learn to perform on the trapeze, and trampoline. There is even instruction in becoming a clown.

Their cuisine is superb because they use native vegetables and fruits. Fish is caught daily and served immediately. Local color and customs are evident in the folklore shows given nightly. Creativity is encouraged in workshops that teach arts and crafts - string necklaces of shells, bone, or leather. There is a course in ceramics, too., Native marine life is studied as well as baking French delicacies. Adventure is found in the overnight trips where all kinds of transportation are used: jeeps, cars, boats, canoes, camels, and even elephants!

# 8

# BED AND BREAKFASTS, INNS AND SMALL HOTELS

*Small hotel at Clapham Common, London, 1984.*

# BED AND BREAKFASTS, INNS AND SMALL HOTELS

Many of us take motor trips and count on travel guides that tell us the best way to reach our destinations, where there are historical memorials, where there is road construction, camping, and picnicking, and where speed laws are strictly enforced.

The most used and popular guides are the AAA TourBooks. Not only the *Triptiks* prepared especially for you whether it is a one day trip or one of several months, but up-to-date maps are furnished. The handy personal booklets are invaluable. Road maps that were once free at gas stations are now expensive. For the AAA member they are free.

Rates are guaranteed at selected hotels and discounts given at these and various tourist attractions. There is a full service Business Travel Department and professionally escorted cruises. There are also fee-free American Express Traveler's Cheques offered. Of course the most reassuring feature is their Emergency Repair Service.

Hotels are rated by stars from ★ that has basic requirements to ★★★★ that usually means a luxury resort. Each year the list is revised and updated. We like AAA hotels that have special value rates advertised in the TourBooks.

The TourBooks give the history, geography, and economy of the states through which you are driving. Information on recreation and points of interest make interesting reading for the passengers.

We try to take back roads and find towns of historical interest. Sometimes time is a factor, and a super highway is the only answer, but if you have time and have done a little research on your own, your trip will be memorable.

If your route is from Florida along the Atlantic Coast, a stop at one of the sea islands can be a treat. Jekyll Island was the home of millionaires like the Goodyears and the Goulds. Now their beautiful mansions remain a part of the Jekyll Island Club Historic District, and one can take a guided tour by tram through the area. The club now owned by Radisson gives AAA rates. We stayed there overnight and found ourselves imagining the past when the great financiers gathered there with their families.

A way of making motor trips interesting is stopping at a country inn. There are guide books for each section of this country describing inns noted for their architectural style, location, furnishings, and history. Most of these have six to eight rooms, some with private baths.

Our first experience visiting one of these was on our way north. West of Thomasville, Georgia, there is an old plantation. By some stroke of luck, it was one of the few untouched by the Civil War. An Englishman has furnished it as it once was with silk drapes, oriental rugs, and antiques. This mansion with its handsome wallpaper, delicate sculptured woodwork, and elegant spiral staircase is well worth traveling miles to see. Our bedroom had a high four postered bed with an embroidered spread that matched the drapes. An antique table held a bowl of fresh fruit.

Breakfast is usually included in these inns, and ours here was in a high ceiling dining room with elaborate crystal candelabra. I especially remember the shirred eggs and hot corn bread served there.

Rates are higher than the usual Bed and Breakfast, but then one is paying for a glimpse of history and beauty recaptured by the owner. Reservations must be made far in advance.

Inns are a business and depend on guests to pay the expenses. They usually have six or more guest rooms and often have a restaurant open to the public. Generally the host lives on the premises.

"Bed and Breakfast" is a private home, and often called a "homestay." All B & B's became popular when people got tired of impersonal motels that were too often expensive even though they were called budget.

I can recall a family trip out west in the forties on which my mother would inspect tourist homes and small hotels often finding many of them had beds infested with bedbugs! With the international travel increasing in the last thirty years, Americans have found bed and breakfast lodging in Great Britain, Ireland, and other parts of the continent, and now are glad that we finally have homestays of our own.

When Harry and I visited Nova Scotia in 1981, there were few motels besides the large government owned hotels. The tourist office had written us of their Farm and Country Vacations. Their booklet listed hosts and their homes. Before we left home, we made reservations at those that most appealed to us. However, when we left the ferry and turned off the main road onto a back country road, Harry was pessimistic. We drove miles before we reached "Island Haven", a white farmhouse encircled by a creek. When Cal and Lorna Watts greeted us, his spirits rose. Cal, a retired navy officer, regaled us at dinner with stories of his experiences.

It was a new experience for us to stay with strangers. The rates were more reasonable than a motel and included breakfast and dinner. Since there were no other guests, the facilities were private.

We stayed two days exploring the wilderness in Cal's canoe. Harry picked apples, dug up vegetables from the garden, and even caught a chicken for dinner while I relaxed in the porch hammock. Isolated as they were, the Watts were eager for company. For us, it was an unique experience in which we learned more about the country and its people, finding out points of interest not listed in any guidebook.

During our three weeks in Nova Scotia, we stopped at other homes, met interesting retired couples, had some good accommodations, and others less than best. One afternoon we stopped at a home where we had reservations. Since it looked deserted, Harry went to the door to investigate. To his dismay, a large Doberman met him halfway up the path, ready to attack. Harry ran back to the car in time to escape, but lost his good hat! Later we called from another home listed in our book, canceling our room despite the hostess protesting her dog was harmless.

Since our visit, Bed and Breakfast places have been screened and are now under the supervision of the Dept. of Tourism (Box 130, Halifax, Nova Scotia, Canada, B3J 2M7). We endorse this program to meet the local people for they are aware of so many attractions not found in a guidebook. Better Bed and Breakfast places are found every year as more people travel to Nova Scotia. It's reassuring to know there is a Tourist Board that has strict standards that must be kept by the hosts.

Now in every state, the Canadian provinces of Alberta, British Columbia, New Brunswick, Ontario, Prince Edward Island, and Quebec, there are listings for B & B homestays.

The four C's of Bed and Breakfast are comfort, cleanliness, cordiality, and cost (fair).

We have found that using B & B's as we go north every year has provided interesting places to see as well as good accommodations in homes along the way.

Our favorite city is Beaufort, S.C. where there are antebellum homes offering guest rooms for tourists. These, overlooking the estuary and sea, have wide verandas and high ceiling rooms with antiques and four postered beds. In North Carolina, an inn that caters to yachtsmen sailing north offers comfortable rooms, and a smorgasbord known for miles around. There are many opportunities to stay at good homestays no matter in which direction you are headed. *Bed & Breakfast U.S.A.*, a guide to tourist homes and guest homes, had been compiled by Betty Rundback and Nancy Kramer and is a most comprehensive guide for travelers wishing to find a good B & B. Single women feel less threatened in this family-type environment where the host and guest are congenial.

At first, it seems strange to sit at a dining table with strangers, and yet have the ambience of a real family. We have marveled at the way everyone talks freely while eating a good breakfast. So many travelers are from different parts of the country that there is always something interesting one can offer that another person hasn't heard of. I can't recall any unpleasant encounters with tourists met in a B & B. The atmosphere is so relaxed with the host setting the tone with his helpfulness and friendliness.

Bed and Breakfast homes offer breakfast, "continental" (fruit rolls, and hot beverage), and "full" (fruit, cereal, eggs, and bacon, breads, and hot beverage.) A few offer other meals at extra cost.

Inns offer a modified American plan (breakfast and dinner included) and an American plan (three meals a day).

Our favorite inn is in Hancock, New Hampshire. The John Hancock Inn is reputed to be the oldest hostelry, operating since 1789. The carriage (social) room has tables made from authentic bellows found in an old blacksmith shop, and the seats are from carriages. Wide board floors and beams that have held the building together for so long are admired by antique lovers. The bedrooms feature antiques, braided rugs, and primitive painting, all early American decor. The inn's garden has vegetables that are served in season. The small town of Hancock has a tranquility hard to find in today's world. A week spent here restored our spirits.

What should you look for in selecting a bed and breakfast guest house? Each state has its own organization that inspects and endorses the best places, but sometimes they are filled and you must select an unrecommended spot.

It is best to make an on-the-spot inspection. Is the bathroom near the bedroom, and how many are using it? Are the beds firm? This is most important for anyone suffering from a bad back. Are there twin or double beds? Is the guest house in a quiet neighborhood, or if on the main street, is there a bedroom available in the back? Do they serve breakfast early?

We found this important since we are early risers and don't like to wait until eight o'clock for a cup of coffee. Is the breakfast, if continental, adequate? A glass of juice, toast, and coffee isn't enough for us, and sometimes the nearest restaurant can be far away. Hosts may own a dog or cat. If you are allergic, it's best to ask when you make your reservation.

Often you can tell by the appearance of a home - lawn littered, peeling paint, and general neglect - that the inside won't be neat and clean.

Inns are generally good, because if the standards are lowered, they will not continue in business. However, a bed board is often necessary to be more comfortable, and if your bedroom is over the bar, you may have trouble sleeping. Some have good meals, others mediocre. Often the atmosphere and added features like fruit and wine in your room, make up for this deficiency. I personally like a balcony or porch off our room.

Pamela Lanier in her *Complete Guide to Bed & Breakfasts, Inns, and Guesthouses,* covers the U.S., Puerto Rico, Virgin Islands, West Indies, Caribbean, Bermuda, and Mexico. According to her, most inns have under thirty guest rooms, while a B & B is a home with three or more rooms in a large house or mansion, with eight or nine guest accommodations, and serves breakfast. Guest Houses are private homes welcoming guests. Some may be contacted directly or reserved through a reservation service organization.

The innkeeper is more than willing to help you with suggestions, but don't expect any personal service. Usually you will have to carry your own suitcase. Since bathrooms are usually shared, it's a courtesy to other guests to remove your toilet articles and towels and leave everything as you found it. If you come in late, try to be quiet and not awaken the other guests and host.

Some B & B hosts are flexible and will have the drip coffee pot ready to plug in, fresh rolls and juice in the refrigerator, and boxes of cereal on the counter. This is especially nice if you are early risers like we are. One place we stayed locked the kitchen and didn't serve anything until 9 a.m.!

Earlier I wrote of the need for peace and tranquility while enjoying a vacation. To many city dwellers, anxious to escape the noise, crowds, and bad weather, a Caribbean cruise may seem the answer, yet often there are so many passengers it's difficult to be alone except in one's cabin.

Religious people look forward to annual stays at their churches' retreats or camps where their spirits gain a sense of renewal, but those who do not attend church need the same kind of haven to help them find peace in this troubled world. Surprisingly, convents, monasteries, and abbeys are now offering their guest rooms to travelers without making any effort to convert them. They just want to offer solitude and scenery to harassed businessmen and housewives.

It might be a Zen monastery in the Catskills, an Episcopal monastery overlooking the Hudson, or a Trappist monastery in Colorado. Participation in religious services is optional but the one honored time is "the Great Silence" between 9 p.m. and 8:15 a.m. The monasteries and convents offer three home-cooked meals a day, quiet, tidy rooms, and charge $50 a night. There are six hundred small monasteries in the U.S. with guest rooms. Some house retired priests, nuns, and other professional church workers. Some of these buildings were once grand mansions with many rooms for guests.

Marcia Kelly and her husband, Jack, have written a book, *Sanctuaries* (Bell Tower, 1991) that is a guide to lodging in monasteries in the Northeast. The book is very popular with those searching for quiet and peace. Often the beautiful setting remote in the hills can give people just what they've been looking for. The Carmelite House of Prayer in Oakville, California, a former family mansion with eleven guest rooms, lies in the Napa Valley.

"I come up here to hear myself think," said Jason Erlicsohn, a 37 year-old banker from San Francisco. From his Spartan room he can also hear a fountain in the monastery courtyard, the clang of the temple bell, and a song from a mockingbird. "I used to go to a health spa when I got stressed out. Now I just sit and listen," he said. "I feel great after my stay here."

There is great contrast between these retreats and modern luxurious houses with their swimming pools and tennis courts. Breakfast is served at a formal dining table where sixteen guests eat a hearty meal of cereal, eggs, homemade muffins, and fresh fruit. There is plenty of hot coffee in the silver urn. The Sisters of St. Birgitta have pledged themselves to make an effort to be hospitable to guests.

"The sisters can't do enough for us," said a retired librarian who lives in Brooklyn and visits the convent for weekends and vacations. "They cook, serve, polish the floors, and pray in the chapel. They even tend nine acres of grounds."

Living in harmony with a religious order must give anyone an inner feeling of contentment. Meditation sessions are not required, but after experiencing even one, a guest must reflect on his or her life and where it is heading.

In addition to taking vows of poverty, chastity, and obedience, the nuns make a real effort to make guests feel welcome. Their day starts at 6:15 a.m. with community prayers, and then their work begins. What examples they set for the guests! Thousands of Americans are planning vacations this year on a higher spiritual plane hoping to find peace and to leave the violence and chaos of the world behind for even a short time. This move toward religious retreats may convert some people to a faith they've rejected or perhaps never had.

For those looking for a small luxury hotel or resort, Pamela Lanier's *Elegant Small Hotels* is a connoisseur's guide that gives lists and descriptions of small hotels in forty states, Puerto Rico, U.S. Virgin Islands, West Indies, Canada, Mexico, Caribbean, and Bermuda. This book is for people of discerning tastes and men traveling on business who want pleasant surroundings in which to work and relax.

"Elegant" means the decor, the atmosphere of a fine residence with beautiful furnishings and an eye to design and color. With this comes little touches like fresh flowers, nightly turn-down (with a chocolate!), overnight shoeshine, luxurious toiletries, and oversized towels.

"Small" means under two hundred guest rooms; most of the ones mentioned are much smaller.

In addition, if one is a business man, he can expect secretarial services on call, telex, computer telecommunications, and a conference room. Most traveling men want to keep physically fit, so they will look for a spa, massage room, swimming pool, and tennis or privileges in a nearby health center.

Of course, a fine cuisine is offered, with a dress code requiring coat and tie for dinner, and only guests are allowed in the dining room.

The concierge will assist you in every way. There is a politeness and attention to detail rarely found in commercial hotels. Service and style is characteristic of these hotels, too.

# 9

# IF WE'RE FLYING, LET'S BE COMFORTABLE

*When you leave your seat, you'll need this.*

# IF WE'RE FLYING, LET'S BE COMFORTABLE

Why do people fly? Often, the countryside is beautiful, and anyone up in an airplane will not see any of it. Unlike a ship or train, there's little chance to move about. You must sit in cramped quarters closer to people than you would wish, especially if they have colds. Reading, watching movies, listening to tapes, and eating are the only diversions.

We have often tallied our expenses when driving to New England from Florida, and, compared with the cost of the airline ticket, it is more expensive to stay overnight at motels or inns. Meals and gas add up, too, so perhaps you fly to save money.

However, the main reason given by most people is they have a vacation of limited duration, and flying is the only way they can reach their destination and have time to enjoy their holiday.

If you are apt to become seasick or car sick from bumpy roads, flying is the only way for you to go. If an airport is near you, there's no problem in connecting with planes in Atlanta or New York.

How do you reach the airport from your home? Taxis are expensive, but driving your own car and parking it at the airport can be expensive, too. There have sprung up Super Shuttles in large cities that are only one third the cost of a taxi.

Airport limousines large enough to accommodate eight to ten passengers are in demand, because they will call for you and deliver you on time for your flight.

We Americans take these large cars or busses for granted, but in England one time, we had difficulty in finding one. Our small English inn, Ebury Court, had a porter who offered to find us transportation to Heathrow. "Did we want a Mercedes or a Rolls?" We were quick to say we wanted the airport limousine, not a private car. He still didn't seem to understand.

"We don't want a car and chauffeur, but a bus that takes tourists to the airport," Harry explained.

The porter scratched his head and seemed deep in thought. Then he clapped his hands. "Blyme," he exclaimed. "You mean the Airbus!"

Nothing could have been more convenient. Our hotel was a block from Victoria Station. The porter piled our luggage on his dolly at the appointed time, and led the way to the Airbus stop near the station.

It's important to call to confirm your flight. Sometimes schedules are changed, and you haven't been notified.

When you order your ticket, get your seat assignment. Aisle seats are popular, because it's easy to get up and stretch now and then. We choose one window seat and one on the aisle hoping that the seat in between may not be booked, and we'll have room to stretch out.

It's easier on your back to carry two small suitcases instead of one large one, if you can't get any Skycap to help you or if you can't find one of the baggage carts.

It's always possible to arrive without your luggage, so it's important to pack toiletries, medicines, a change of underwear, and nightgown or pajamas in your carry on for an emergency.

Clearly printed covered tags should be attached to all your luggage, and just for quick identification, we use bows of red ribbon. It's important to go directly to the baggage claim area to make sure no one takes your suitcases. Many of those small plaid bags are easily confused unless you check.

Our Aunt Sarah arrived in Chicago for a visit after attending a granddaughter's wedding in Connecticut. The first thing she did was open her plaid bag to show us her lovely gown for the wedding. Imagine her dismay when the contents revealed a baseball bat, soiled underwear, sneakers, and a boy's baseball cap!

She called the airport and within an hour, her suitcase arrived, and the other was returned.

In our carry-ons we include our cameras and film, but insist that the attendant check them by hand. X-rays can fog your film. In some countries like Italy and France, they will insist everything be X-rayed because of terrorists.

We always carry a lead-shield bag in which our film is stored. That way we can be sure of no damage.

After some unhappy hours spent in crowded Kennedy Airport, we always try to avoid New York. It's not easy when your destination is United Kingdom or Europe. Planning a trip to Lisbon, Portugal, we saw an ad in the travel section of our paper. It read, "Right from your door to Lisbon, Portugal!" Interested, we decided to take this flight via Atlanta to Toronto, Canada, and then across on Air Canada. During our three hour layover in Toronto, we had a dinner in a new airport hotel. Air Canada proved spacious, uncrowded, and comfortable. Alcoholic drinks and wine were complimentary. It was by far the most pleasant flight we had to Europe.

We were delighted that many package tours that include airfare now will allow "Land Only" for tourists wishing to leave from an airport closer to their homes. You can find an economy flight that leaves a city near you and join your group overseas.

Since we live in Florida, most of the planes we take, stop in Atlanta. Once I complained to a man seated next to me about having to change planes in Atlanta. "Why, everyone goes through Atlanta," he said. "They say if you want to go heaven, you must stop there!" Another version: "They say whether you're going to heaven or hell, you have to go through Atlanta!"

A month ago we found our connecting plane required an hour's walk through the Atlanta airport. Our travel agent hadn't known this. If she had, she could have arranged for a reservation for us on the mini-bus that carries passengers from plane to plane. Luckily it was not filled and we were able to climb aboard, but the driver cautioned us to plan ahead as he usually had room only for those with reservations. If you are on a tour or a part of a cruise group, someone at the airport will carry a sign with the name of your tour or ship to direct you in which direction to go.

Stop overs or delays between planes can be annoying, but it's best just to accept these and try to relax. Many enjoy looking at items in the gift shop or browsing at the magazine stand. TV sets at the airport are there to entertain you. In foreign airports, tax free items usually mean lower prices and often make ideal gifts for friends at home. If you are on a budget flight, your lunch may only be crackers and a soft drink, so it may be worthwhile to have something to eat at the airport cafeteria. Bars are popular. You can spend your time having a beer while talking to a fellow passenger. Your traveling group may have some bridge players, so having a deck of cards in your purse will help start a game. I find working crosswords is a great time filler.

Flying is more stressful than most people realize. If you're flying in a Boeing 747 at an altitude of 12,000 feet, the cabin pressure inside is what it would be at 1500 to 2000 feet above sea level. Since most live near sea level, this requires a lot of body adjustment.

How can you make your air trip more comfortable? Here are a few suggestions: drink fruit juice and water (coffee and tea act as diuretics); don't smoke; eat lightly before leaving home and very little during the flight; have a blanket nearby or carry a sweater and slipper-socks in your carry on. If you suffer from earaches while flying, take an antihistamine or decongestant forty-five minutes before takeoff. For a long flight, put up your feet on a small travel bag, and use a tube of moisturizer to cool your face since the plane air will be very dry. One suggestion is to spray your face with water from an atomizer like models do.

Some airplane trips can be especially enjoyable if the flight captain points out interesting places visible on a clear day. Recently our captain pointed out the island of Chincoteague off the coast of Virginia and remarked that the ponies there are the descendants of horses that survived the shipwreck of a Spanish galleon in the 16th century. On that remarkably clear day, we saw New York and Philadelphia. Delta has a map of its routes in its *Sky Magazine* as do other airlines in their publications. It's interesting to trace the route you are flying. Every now and then walk up and down the aisle to help your circulation.

Sometimes when one is flying a new route, a landing can be unexpectedly breath-taking. Our destination was Madeira, a small mountainous island off the coast of Africa. Our jet flew down giving us a glimpse of mountains, terraced vineyards and fruit orchards. There seemed to be no level ground. Finally, we coasted down the short runway and came to a stop just a few feet from the sea! Loud gasps came from the passengers, then shouts of relief and joy. Later we learned that the year before, a plane had slipped off into the sea causing some fatalities. Since then a few feet had been added for safety's sake.

Harry reminds me of the shock I gave him the time our small plane left St. Thomas in the Virgin Islands and landed on the deserted beach of Rockefeller's Little Dix Bay. He thought our plane would land on a conventional airstrip.

Sometimes there's an element of risk in taking small commuter planes. The most frightening flight of our lives was in a Comanche flying from Miami to Sarasota, Florida. When we came in from our overseas flight and confirmed our tickets, we should have been alerted when the attendant said, "How much do you weigh?" I don't usually give that kind of information to even my best friend! Harry looked at me, and asked, "Are you sure we shouldn't take a jet to Tampa and then a limousine home?" I shook my head. I wasn't afraid of being one of the few passengers on a light plane, but later, I regretted my decision. Our pilot apparently had not paid much attention to the weather report, and later we found very rough going as the end of a hurricane made its way north. There was a pilot, a co-pilot, and five passengers, all young, besides ourselves. After our plane fell around one hundred feet, conversation stopped and from then on, all of us prayed. Afterward, Harry confessed our affairs were not in good shape; we had talked about having a Living Will, and I regretted not writing more to our daughter. It seemed an eternity before Harry said, "You can open your eyes now. I see the lights of Sarasota."

Before this experience, I had visited our daughter in Ketcham, Idaho. It was January, and the only way out when the snow was six feet deep was to fly to Twin Falls. Our single engine plane flew over the Sawtooth Mountain Range in a blinding snowstorm! You can be sure my life passed in review, and praying was in order. Later we read in the Idaho newspaper that the owner of the airline had taken the flight after ours, and his plane had crashed!

Even on jumbo jets, there is adventure. I have never been on a hijacked plane, but I have had to bypass Chicago, as it was not possible to land, and to spend the night in Detroit with a passenger I had just met. An unexpected treat awaited us when our plane arrived in Denver. Our flight to Yellowstone had been cancelled because of snow. Our airline not only provided lodging in our favorite Brown Palace Hotel, but dinner and breakfast, too.

I could never understand why overseas planes don't fly in the morning in time for dinner in London. It's nice to know that now two airlines, British Airways and American, fly from New York in the morning, arriving in England in the early evening. But most of the charter flights still leave the U.S. in the evening.

Maybe you are like me. I can't sleep much on an overseas flight. I cover my eyes with air travel blinkers, and listen to the music coming through my earphones, but time passes very slowly. I envy passengers who curl up under a blanket right after the sign "No seat belts" is on and are not heard from until breakfast is being served.

I've read somewhere that jet lag lowers our mental and physical efficiency by up to twenty percent. There's supposed to be a twenty-four hour recovery time for every two hour time difference. I change my watch when I board the plane, and that helps, but when we arrive in London and have to cope with a strange hotel and too many tourists, I invariably have a headache that stays with me for two or three days.

Of course, taking the four hour trip on the Concord is the answer, but few of us can afford the stiff tariff. Most take Apex (Advance Purchase Excursion), a round trip ticket paid for in advance and discounted from normal full fare.

Recently, a friend bought a special excursion ticket available to senior citizens allowing her to make two round trip flights within a certain time. The airline ticket man advised her to hang on to her ticket. She flew to Denver to visit her family and then later to New England to visit friends. When she picked up her reservations for the last trip, the agent asked for her excursion ticket. Alas, she had discarded it in Denver, and had to pay fifty dollars more for this second flight.

On long flights to the Far East and to Africa, there are usually two or three stops to break up the time and give you a chance to walk about, and even to rest, if it's overnight. Often this is time well spent, because arriving exhausted at your destination often means you'll need more time to recover before you can begin to enjoy your vacation.

Flying has a lot to recommend it. The speed and ease with which you travel may make up for additional time in which you ordinarily would be enjoying the scenery, and learning more about the country.

So remember, when you board your plane, and are settled in your seat, take off your shoes, elevate your feet, and try to relax. Eat sparingly, and drink lots of water and fruit juices. Dream about the wonders you will see, and if returning, think of the good times to remember.

# 10

# HOW'S THE FOOD?

*The Barenplatz, Berne, Switzerland, 1984.*

# HOW'S THE FOOD?

One of the most important questions travelers ask is "How's the food?" For women, embarking on any trip means a vacation from cooking, planning menus, and trips to the local supermarket. The daily grind of setting the table, serving the food, clearing, and then washing the dishes, and pans (even if you're lucky to have a dishwasher, there are still some utensils that must be hand washed) is something every woman and man wishes to be free of, if only for a few days. There is a constant worry about increasing costs of fruits, vegetables, and meat, not to mention dairy products. When one signs up for a tour or extended trip, the thought of leaving all the daily household responsibilities behind makes one glow with happy anticipation.

Not only food preparation and everything that goes into making a meal encourages one to leave home, but the mundane, daily jobs of making beds, vacuuming, and dusting are additional incentives. So a person embarking on a vacation leaves this all behind, and since it is hoped he or she is healthy, appetites play a major part in enjoyment of time away from home.

Food! The person who sets forth with a thirst to learn more about food in other places, many of them foreign to him or his background, will find sampling menus other than those to which he is accustomed, a great revelation and, many times, a rare treat. Of course, there are now McDonald's around the world and in our great hotel chains, an American can always find a hamburger and milk shake. Many carry their eating tastes with them and so miss adventures in eating.

I am reminded of one day in Thessalonki, Greece. Harry and I had just explored a medieval church. It was noon, my husband reminded me, and his stomach told him it was time to have lunch. We had come into port on our Yugoslavian freighter, the *Zvir*, and were walking about the old city completely on our own. "But all the signs are upside down, and we don't know which building is a restaurant. We can't even recognize a hotel!"

Harry stared across the street at a storefront. "But I feel sure that's a bank over there," he said. "The men have on business suits and are wearing ties." Harry is a retired banker and I guess it takes one to know one. At any rate, we crossed the street and I waited outside while Harry inquired about where we could find some lunch. He was gone a long time. Finally, I looked through the window and saw Harry standing beside a tight circle of men. All were gesticulating with their arms, as if they were arguing. Finally, they seemed to reach an agreement. Harry came out smiling, followed by three men. One whistled loudly with his fingers and a taxi appeared around the corner. He opened the car door, and helped me get in. "Where are we going?" I asked, a bit confused.

"Wait and see," Harry said smugly. It wasn't long before we arrived back on the dock area. The taxi stopped in front of a long building and we went inside. To our relief, tables with white tablecloths and waiters bustling about carrying trays loaded with food greeted us, and it wasn't long before we were seated among people who dressed and talked like natives, looking at long menus. Harry shook his head. "It's all Greek to me!" We both started to laugh recognizing an old phrase that had never been used more aptly.

The man at the next table turned and grinned. "You must be Americans. Would you allow me to order some of the best dishes for you?"

We nodded. "Wonderful," I said, "Neither my husband nor I have the faintest idea what's on this menu."

Our Greek friend summoned our waiter and spoke rapidly in Greek. Then he turned to us. "Once I was in your country, and a kind gentleman helped me. I like especially your mashed potatoes." He told us he was there on business, and his home was in Athens.

What a feast we had! First, there was dolmades, vine leaves stuffed with rice, meat and onion, very good. I had asked for moussaka because I'm fond of eggplant. Harry liked the spinakopitta, a spinach and goat cheese pie. For dessert, we had baklava. Our friend ordered a delicious wine, Porto Carras. Our meal at Olympus Naoussa was a memorable experience.

Many of our gastronomic adventures seemed to have happened at noontime. After a morning of sightseeing and exploring, we become hungry and try to choose restaurants based on recommendation in our guidebook, or made by some knowledgeable person we'd met.

In Lisbon, Portugal, our first visit was the Gulbenkian Museum where many paintings from Leningrad's Hermitage are displayed. Opposite the museum and its lovely park is a restaurant called O Paco and known for its literary clientele. It seemed to be a favorite of local gentry, but there was no way to tell which ones were writers or poets.

As we entered, we passed a long counter displaying all kinds of fish: lobster, crab, clams, and mussels on ice. We sat in a booth, and before we ordered anything, six or more small dishes were set before us. Appetizers, we thought, and being hungry, ate them all. Then a waiter came, carrying a huge tray loaded with fish. Harry had seen a plate of broiled sardines, much larger than ours, and ordered these. The clams appealed to me. To our surprise, large bowls of soup called *caldierada* much like our bouillabaisse came first. After this course, our appetite was somewhat abated before the main entrée arrived. Maderia wine was suggested, and it proved very good. To Harry's surprise, when the check came, it included all the appetizers. Later, we found the custom was to choose which one we wanted, if any. The entire cost was still lower than any such luncheon we might have had at home.

In this same city, a restaurant that had to be reached by elevator appealed to us. It was located on a higher level than the main street, so that the view of the old section, Alfama, was magnificent. A Quinta was an old restaurant run by a Portuguese family. There, we sampled small clams, ameijoas, that were delicious.

Our first visit to England held some surprises in the food area. Famous eating places like Rules, Sherlock Holmes, and the Old Cheshire Cheese served good roast beef, but the vegetables were overcooked. Bubble and Squeak, a combination of onions and beans, was different tasting. Our favorites were mutton pie, Yorkshire pudding, and trifle. However, we didn't care for our beer or ale tepid. The English think we ruin our drinks by adding ice!

Harry recalls one of the strangest meals in his life. During World War II, his orders were to ride by Tibetan pony from the southern part of Yunan in China to the Salween River front. The American and Chinese officers accompanied by interpreters threaded their way through the high mountain passes; each rider was protected in the rear by a foot soldier who walked, jogged, or ran the entire journey.

A Chinese general welcomed them at their destination. It was necessary to bend low because the doorway was under six feet (Harry is six feet, four inches.) The dining area was screened off by a cloth over the doorway. In the center of the room was a large table on which lay chop sticks, and a mound of dried, salted grasshoppers and ancient eggs. These were the appetizers. Then, the host became animated as his wife entered the room. Harry first noticed her small bound feet, and that she was carrying a tray on which there was a steaming pot. In it was a whole chicken. Its head hung over one side, its two mud-incrusted feet over the other. Hungry though the Americans were, this bird, obviously not eviscerated, filled them with dismay.

As if sensing their embarrassment, the general picked up his chop sticks and deftly slit off the tender portions of the chicken. He helped himself and then gestured for the guest to help themselves. They were so hungry, Harry recalls, that they devoured the entire meal - bean sprouts, cabbage, and bird. Not to mention the ancient eggs and fried grasshoppers. Behind each guest stood peasant soldiers who serve hot green tea. It was an experience never to be forgotten.

In Sogndal, Norway, where we spent a week in the Elderhostel program, we grew used to having raw fish and different cheeses for breakfast. The same was true of our Norwegian freighter, the *Salvador*, but they included caviar.

In England, we grew accustomed to tea in the mid afternoon, but were surprised to find recently that in the large London hotels "high tea" was being replaced by the cocktail hour. We love the sandwiches and all kinds of cakes and scones offered at "high tea."

I wish our hotels would adopt a New Zealand custom of having hotel rooms with refrigerators where fresh milk is placed each day. There are also a burner and tea kettle with coffee and tea supplied, and occasionally, tea biscuits.

I never had a pocket sandwich until we arrived in Brisbane, Australia. These are sold on the street and are very tasty and hearty with hot meat and gravy inside the pastry.

There is nothing more tempting or fattening than the Sacher Torte, named for the famous hotel in Vienna, unless it's the strudel at the Cirq in the Bristol Hotel of that same city. Chocolate in Switzerland is a temptation, but when it comes to those cream-filled cakes, *Schfferhauserzungen*, I throw my diet to the winds.

A friend visited Port Said, Egypt. As they were driven to their hotel, Evelyne noticed native women rolling and patting flat cakes in an area infested with flies. Dust covered everything. "What are they making?" she said.

"Bread" was the guide's reply.

Later when Evelyne was offered rolls, she refused. The memory of that native bread was fresh in her mind. "In Egypt, I suffered from culture shock," she confessed. "I never realized how important our health regulations are. We take for granted that everything must be sanitary and clean."

Large cruise ships are like deluxe, floating hotels, and the quantity of food needed for so many passengers requires careful planning and ordering before sailing. Each ship vies with a sister ship in its cuisines, trying to be first in the ice sculpture that sets the tone of the buffet, and in making creations of chocolate and sugar. The chefs on our ship were young Austrian and Germans, artists in making anything from petit fours to fish platters featuring whole salmon.

An hour before serving, photographers were allowed to view their masterpieces and capture them on camera. Windmills of Swiss chocolate, pastry in the form of small animals, towers made from croissants - each time the motif was different, and the display mouth-watering.

One day, our chefs gave a workshop for passengers and revealed some of their secrets. Surprisingly much of the decoration was nothing but food coloring and sugar paste, but the artistic way in which everything was placed on the platter or plate was wonderful!

One specialty was chocolates, and they showed their special molds for making the outside covering. Then there were many fillings added.

Because Desert Storm was over and we were going home, there was a hamburger made out of two macaroons with chocolate as a filling. An added touch was a tiny American flag stuck in it.

A tradition of the Royal Viking Line is for one evening of a cruise segment to have an impressive parade of waiters coming into a dark dining room, holding high a platter of flaming Alaska (a cake filled with ice cream, covered with meringue, and surrounded by liqueur that is set afire.) Adding to the occasion is pomp and circumstance music.

Seasoned travelers heed the rule, "Eat no green vegetables or fresh fruit you can't peel." This should be observed especially in third world countries. Mexico is noted for the traveler's Montezuma Revenge. This illness, usually resulting in diarrhea, is caused by drinking the local water and breaking the above rule concerning fresh vegetable and fruits. To avoid any discomfort, we brushed our teeth using beer for a rinse, ate cooked vegetables, and bananas. Our only drink was beer. Those in charge of cruise excursions will caution passengers about eating ashore, recommending lunch on the ship instead.

The freighters we traveled on had excellent food. It was plain but well cooked. There were strict rules on how it was prepared and served. The same was true of bed and breakfasts, and inns. Grand Circle representatives advised us in the country we were visiting and listed restaurants which had good food.

# 11

# SNORKELING, BARGING AND RAFTING

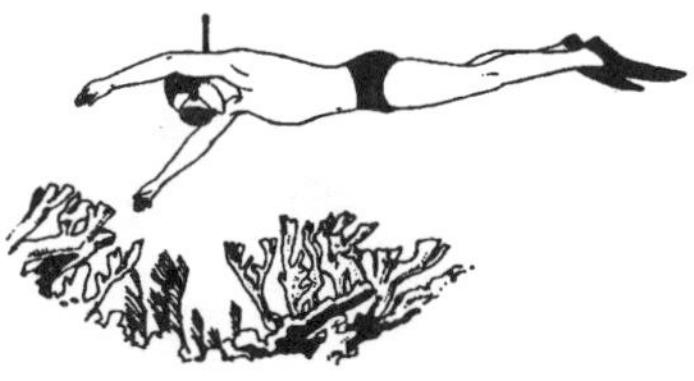

*Along the canal of Burgundy, 1984.*

# SNORKELING, BARGING AND RAFTING

Years ago, we vacationed in St. Croix. One morning we boarded a giant catamaran and sailed over to Buck Island where the Captain told us there was an underwater trail that had types of coral marked and unusual fish. A glass bottom boat would take us over this wonder garden, but when we reached it, some of our passengers took the snorkeling gear offered and prepared to explore with a guide taking charge.

Jacque Cousteau is our favorite, and we try not to miss any of the *Calypso's* adventures. But his men were scuba divers and spent a long time underwater. Snorkeling was different. Anyone who can swim will find it an easy and exciting sport.

Always eager to try something new, we followed the guide's instructions, first breathing through our mouth, and then, after masks were fitted to our head, we spit into them to clear the glass, fastened the J-shaped tubes (the snorkels) to them, and inserted the soft rubber bits in our mouths. Then, we put on our rubber fins which seemed clumsy, but in the water by doing a flutter kick, we could move with speed and ease.

The next thing we knew we were in the water, face downward, seeing the world below so clearly. Objects underwater are twenty-five percent larger when seen through a mask because of the refraction of light in the water. At first, water flooded my mask because the end of my snorkel went below the surface. I didn't become panicky because our leader had me raise my head and pull the bottom of my mask away from my face letting the water escape. After readjusting my mask, I became relaxed as I breathed through my snorkel.

What an exciting experience it was to move along the trail, holding onto the leader's hand as he led the way over beautiful ferns and sea anemones. And the fish! Schools of black and white Spadefish, yellow Butterflyfish, black and yellow Sergeant-majors-the list goes on. My *Guide to Fish Species* helped me identify later what I had seen. The dark French Angelfish, the orange Filefish, and the red and white Squirrel fish swam so close to us we could have reached out and touched them. The underwater trail was well marked with signs designating the various kinds of coral; brain, staghorn, elkhorn, and star are so aptly named because of the shapes. This experience opened a new world of sea life that we'd often wondered about when fishing.

I had to guard against flooding my mask because I wear contact lenses and I might lose them. Harry found he could wear his glasses inside the mask.

From that St. Croix adventure, we went on to snorkel in many places. Some of our young friends urged us to dive below the surface, but professional lessons were needed for this and we realized there was an element of danger involved in clearing the masks, and pressure on the ears and sinuses.

One vacation took us to Cozumel, Yucatan, a resort relatively unknown when we first visited it. Just beyond our hotel and the narrow white beach there lay an area offshore abounding in schools of tropical fish. It was a perfect place to snorkel. The current carried us down the beach as we found more and more exotic fish. Because there was a danger of our backs becoming sunburned, we wore T-Shirts.

I liked to put on my fins in the shade of a palm tree, but this meant walking in them toward the water, an awkward procedure. I finally found that walking backward is the only way, as experienced snorkelers know.

Many years later, a Caribbean cruise took me, our daughter, and grandchildren to Cozumel for a one day stopover. While some passengers rented taxis to explore the small island, I introduced my family to snorkeling. There was the same stand on the beach where we could rent equipment. The children were excellent swimmers, and it wasn't long before they adjusted to breathing through their mouths and snorkels. Most of the day was spent drifting along the shore, watching the schools of fish.

Once I had to clear my mask in deep water, snorkeling in Trunk Bay, St. John. To my dismay, it slipped out of my hand and sank out of sight. Luckily, the lifeguard came to my aid and swam out to retrieve it. The mask belonged to him so he had good reason to dive for it.

Another time we had a scary experience while visiting at the Lawrence Rockefeller's Little Dix Bay Resort, Virgin Gorda. One day, a barbecue on a remote beach was held for guests. The cove where everyone swam was pleasant, but there were not enough fish to make snorkeling interesting. We were the only ones who'd brought snorkeling gear, and soon we found a narrow passage that led to the sea beyond. There were many fish here, and we must have swum farther than we realized. The shore was dense with palm trees and very wild. Harry motioned for me to follow him back through the passage. To our consternation, we found the tide that had taken us out had changed, and the strong current made tough going. Exhausted, we kept our fins going in flutter kicks, and securing our masks and snorkels to our heads, we swam as hard as we could. After what seemed a long time, the lagoon where the other guests were swimming loomed ahead. Never was there a more welcome sight! To our amazement, no one had missed us since we were all strangers having just arrived the day before. That was a good lesson for us not to swim away from a group without notifying anyone. It is easy to be carried away with all the sights down under, and not to watch how far away you've gone.

Near our Florida home is John Pennekamp Coral Reef State Park in Key Largo. It is our first continental underseas park and is named for the associate editor of the *Miami Herald*. The park stretches twenty-one miles parallel to Key Largo, and is three and a half miles wide.

The park's boat, *The Infante*, takes snorkelers out twelve miles to the coral reef.

The snorkeling there was breathtaking because we swam in sixty foot depths, and the fish were large barracuda, sharks, and giant sea turtles. There were reef fish, too, and forty-one varieties of coral in flowerlike formations. There were also the hulks of old sailing wrecks.

A park ranger was in charge of the snorkeling. Some swimmers had never worn masks before and being unfamiliar with the procedure and equipment, they became panicky and returned to the diving platform.

Weren't we frightened to have sharks swimming below us? A park official told us there was no danger since the large fish fed at night. In the history of the park, no one had been attacked. I should add that there were professional divers there to help snorkelers.

Our last snorkeling experience was this year when we boarded a giant catamaran, the *Quicksilver*, and left Cairns, Australia for the Great Barrier Reef. This remarkable stretch of coral is vulnerable because it is being eaten by the crown-of-thorns starfish. It wasn't long before we slipped off the landing platform and began to explore, noticing the spectacular staghorn coral and fish like Yellowtail, Bonita, Wrasse, and Goatfish swimming among the brain coral. It's hard to imagine that there are twenty-six hundred individual reefs and about three hundred islands, the largest complex of coral reefs in the world.

Snorkeling is for all ages, as long as you can swim a little. It will give you an intimate contact with the underwater realm that viewing from a glass bottom boat or the TV screen can't duplicate.

The equipment costs very little. The masks should have shatter proof glass and made watertight by a rubber skirt. No plastic should be used and the plates should not be made of tinted glass. The most expensive mask costs $18. The snorkel is made of hard rubber and a soft rubber bit, and costs around $2.50. Snorkels with ping-pong balls and attachments should not be used.

It's best to wear the full shoe type fin of flexible rubber, and it should fit comfortably. They cost about $8.

There are some rules that should be observed both for your enjoyment and safety:

1. Never dive alone!
2. Put up your diving flag, so boats will be aware of you.
3. Be sure to attach your snorkel to your mask.
4. Spit into your mask to defog it and test for leaks.
5. Learn to breathe through your mouth.
6. Learn how to clear your snorkel.
7. Learn how to clear your mask if it's flooded.
8. While you're snorkel cruising, flippers must be submerged.

If you are adventurous, take a course from a certified diver. Never dive beyond the depth of twenty feet. A good handbook for snorkelers is Capt. Steve Klem's book, *Snorkeling For Everyone*, Key Largo, Florida.

There are certain menacing creatures the snorkeler should be aware of. One is the sea urchin. If you are snorkeling in shallow water, it's easy to touch the sea urchin's spine as it's sharp as a needle. Sometimes it's difficult to pull out, and it can be very painful. Another danger is the Portuguese man-of-war which floats and has long, ribbon-like tentacles that sting. Don't swing your arms or you may be stung more. Coral is deceiving. Fire coral is mustard brown in color and if you touch it, you'll have cuts and abrasions that will take weeks to heal.

Jellyfish are not as dangerous as the man-of-war but should be avoided because they sting, too. The cone shell is poisonous. Don't handle it or let your body be in a position where the stinger can be thrust into you. Stingrays are only evident in August or September and lie near the shore under the sand. It's best to shuffle into the water, so that you don't encounter the ray's sting. The best advice I think is, "Live and Let Live." If you respect underwater creatures, and don't act aggressively toward them, you'll have little trouble.

There are cruises now for snorkelers only. Each fall, Quark Expeditions offers a variety of special adventure cruises aboard small ships for divers and snorkelers only. Other snorkeling cruises are planned for the Galapagos Islands, the Red Sea, and the Solomon Islands. For information, write Salen Lindblad Cruising, 113 E. 55th St., New York, NY 10022 or call 1-800-223-5688.

If you want to go down to 150 feet, you might be interested in the Atlantis fleet. These huge vessels sail among the fish like giant white whales giving the passengers an eye-to-eye view of many sea creatures. These Atlantis submarines now operate regularly from ports on Grand Cayman Island, Barbados, and St. Thomas in the Caribbean; Oahu and Hawaii in the Hawaiian Islands; and Guam in the Pacific. The two on Grand Cayman accommodate twenty-five passengers.

Once you learn how to snorkel, you'll have a wonderful time wherever there is water. You don't have to travel far to try out your equipment, and see what's below, even if it's a turtle!

★★★★

The French impressionists, Renoir and Monet, found inspiration for their landscapes by floating down rivers in small boats, dropping anchor when the light was right and the setting to their liking.

As an artist, this leisurely way of seeing the countryside appealed to me. Harry, a photographer, was equally enthusiastic about taking a river boat.

Friends told us about barges that explored Burgundy, so it wasn't long before we signed up to board the *Janine,* a barge 126 feet long that carried twenty-four passengers. What we didn't expect was all the comforts she afforded, or that she would be so attractively furnished. It was a floating hotel with all the amenities.

What a way to sightsee at one or two miles an hour! The passing scenery with its medieval towns and villages held many surprises. There were numerous locks and time enough to talk to the keepers and local farmers. Once we were lucky enough to meet a local lord of the manor who was as interested in us as we were in him. We welcomed a chance to try our college French and found that unlike the busy Parisians, these rural people listened patiently to what we were trying to say.

While Harry was making films of our trip, I didn't lose any opportunity to sketch the ancient churches with their slender spires and the cottages among crumbling fortifications.

Since the *Janine* carried bicycles, we spent part of every morning cycling down the towpath along the rivers and canals. I thought this daily routine of exercise would cause me to lose weight, but, alas, when we followed our chef ashore he bought French pasteries that proved my undoing. His meals were as delicious as in any gourmet restaurant, and served in a saloon with paneled walls and plush banquettes as nice as any fine auberge. Best of all was being able to see the passing scenery through oversized windows.

Harry and I shared a comfortable cabin heated and air-conditioned, carpeted, and attractively decorated.

The crew of eight men knew their French history and, especially, about Burgandy's wineries and such world famous vinters as Clos-Vougeot, Nuits St. George, Geverey-Chambertin, and Beaune.

As we sailed from Dijon to Lyon, we had opportunities to taste-test a wine and then sample it again back on our barge. The highlight was our visit to Beaune where the hospital Hotel-Dieu, built in 1450, had become financially independent because the chancellor of Burgundy deeded his vineyards to it. The plantation was assigned to local growers in a profit-sharing arrangement. Every year there is a spectacular wine auction that attracts connoisseurs from all over the world.

At the end of our six day cruise, my sketchbook was filled with scenes of old men in faded jeans playing boules, the canal with its flocks of brown ducks and banks of wildflowers, the Charollais cattle grazing in the pastures; no wonder Renoir was inspired! We'll never forget the cool cellars in the ancient chateaux where we tasted wine, and then our return to our barge for an English afternoon tea.

Now there are barge cruises offered in England and in Holland, a six day trip from Amsterdam to Marken. In conjunction with American Airlines, the company of Abercrombie & Kent offers three and six day barge cruises in England and France. The number of passengers varies from four to twenty-two. Those carrying more passengers are Hotel Barges; the others are for charter. The prices are all inclusive. Bicycles, sightseeing, taxes, wine, and liquors are part of the cost. There is a low season, April 11 to April 28, October 17 to November 10, and a high one, May 2 to October 13. Costs vary depending on the number of passengers, the luxuries offered, and the gourmet dining. We consulted Kris, our travel agent, who made arrangements and reservations for us.

Hot air ballooning is now popular and spaces may be reserved on various barges twice a week during a six night program.

We did not have a chance to go up in a balloon, but our friends said it was an exciting adventure. The balloons are as tall as a ten story building, and their gondolas carry six to ten people. Four is the minimum. They float across vineyards, chateaux, and woodlands, sometimes drifting low, almost touching treetops. A station wagon followed the balloon's course (which may vary depending on the wind), and arrived just as our friends were climbing out of the gondola. Cheese, French bread, and wine was set out on the tailgate, and the farmers working in the field were invited to join them. The 1991 cost of a hot air balloon trip is $200. The trip lasts about an hour.

New with Abercrombie & Kent is a helicopter charter. When their barge, the *Fleur De Lys*, ends her trip in Nancy, you can transfer to a helicopter and fly to Paris.

Elderhostel offers a two week stay in France with the first week spent on a barge touring Burgundy. In addition to spacious quarters and excellent meals, there are demonstrations of French cooking. This cruise is along the Canal of Burgundy following the valleys of the rivers Ouche and Saone. Included are lectures on history of the Middle Ages when the Valois dukes were independent and gave us rich architectural masterpieces.

Traveling by barge gives one freedom of movement and is very relaxing. No one is pressuring you to get up at a certain time to catch a bus or plane. You literally float along, enjoying the scenery and absorbing the atmosphere. Exercise, either walking or bicycling, can be done on towpaths without danger of traffic and often becomes a real adventure meeting local people and seeing how they live.

For anyone interested in history or architecture, these trips afford much to learn and see. For photography or painting, barge travel offers time and opportunity to capture ancient landscapes, medieval chateaux, and cathedrals. Wine connoisseurs will especially appreciate their experiences visiting wine cellars and test-tasting world famous vintages. The serenity and peace of mind gained from a week of sailing through vineyards and meadows, far from the noise and confusion of big cities, makes barge traveling well worthwhile. We found this the answer when our batteries needed charging.

★★★★

Rafting in a rubber raft down rapids can be exciting. Our trip down the Green River near Vernal, Utah proved thrilling enough for me. There were twenty people that boarded our rubber raft; the orange life jackets in the red raft made a colorful sight. To our surprise many of the passengers had white hair and looked to be in their sixties and seventies. That these older people could risk such a trip reassured me, for I was nervous and reluctant to go along.

Harry, excited at the prospect of using his new camcorder, sat in the middle, but stood during most of the trip. He was the only one who didn't get wet! River water, the color of café au lait, washed over us before we'd gone ten feet. The man in charge of the expedition sat in the bow, barking orders to the man in the stern. By his exasperation, it was evident the stern man was inexperienced and often unable to avoid hitting boulders. The oldest people sat in the bow plainly enjoying the rough ride, but I didn't. It wasn't until we reached home and looked at our movies of the trip that I saw the canyons through which we had rafted.

It was an eventful day. The only break was stopping for a picnic lunch on a flat rock beside the river. There was neither room nor time to stretch ourselves before climbing back onto our raft. Muddy water splashed and often covered me as our craft hit big boulders and slipped off into a deep trough. Most of the passengers screamed with excitement as we were propelled along making me more and more uneasy.

When we finally reached our destination, I stumbled ashore, so relieved to be safe at last, that I choked back tears. Most of the others shook the crewman's hands, ecstatic about their experience. The senior group, it seemed, were going on to Yellowstone Park where they would man concessions.

I thought this would be my one and only rafting trip, but later, when we vacationed in the Tetons, everyone we spoke to raved about the Snake River trip down to Jackson.

Harry convinced me there were no rapids and that a naturalist, a Park Ranger, would accompany us. The boats were small with a maximum of six people.

This proved to be my kind of rafting for we glided down a wide river of clear water with the silence broken only by our guide who pointed out a bald eagle's nest and now and then beaver's dams. The snow-capped Rockies on our right and the National Elk Refuge, where large herds of elk grazed on our left was a scene we'll never forget. An occasional bugle by a bull elk was a thrilling sound. I am sure those wishing for a thrill would prefer white water rafting, but for me, drifting down the tranquil Snake River was much more enjoyable.

# 12

# HOW TO GET THE MOST OUT OF YOUR TRIP

*At a café in Baden-Bei-Vien, 1984.*

# HOW TO GET THE MOST OUT OF YOUR TRIP

Travel enriches your life and enlarges your horizon. In newspapers, a familiar name, or a place where you've been will suggest an experience or an acquaintance. With new eyes, you'll look at your surroundings, thankful your lot is so much better than those of other countries.

TV travelogues cover various vacation areas, and usually there is one that interests you.

Before these were popular, we met a writer who was so enthusiastic about the ruins in Yucatan that we felt inspired to go there. After we read Eric Thompson's account in the library and heard what hardship had befell this English archeologist, the best authority on Mayan culture, and his artist companion, Frederick Catherwood, we flew to Merida for a month's stay, lots of time to explore the ruins of Uxmal and Chichen Itza.

Something else may spark your interest and desire to see the area. Our daughter worked at

Yellowstone Park one summer. The reported summer crowds had kept us away, but now there was a personal reason to visit. September had few tourists and while we were there, it even snowed. We'll never forget the sound of the elk's bugle and roar of the rushing river. After you've made the decision about where to go, necessary arrangements are made through your travel agent. From the brochure, be sure to note what's included in your tour. Are you expected to have some meals at your own expense? If so, it's important to check your Fodor or Frommer guide for recommended restaurants in that area. Be aware of what sort of accommodations you can expect. An economy package will provide modest rooms, and a deluxe tour should arrange for luxurious quarters. Usually, you get what you pay for, but sometimes it's a pleasant surprise when the small room you expected turns out to be large with amenities as nice as an expensive tour. This, however, is not likely to happen on most package tours of Europe.

Your travel agent will tell you the shots needed, mainly for overseas travel and especially for third world countries. They are not covered by Medicare, and some are expensive. Take water purification tablets, and only drink mineral water, having the bottle opened in front of you. Never drink tap water or water with ice in it. In Mexico, we brush our teeth with beer. It's best to refrain from eating salads and dairy products if you think there in inadequate refrigeration.

Ask your doctor for a list of practitioners in the country you are visiting. Another way is to contact a non-profit organization called *International Association for Medical Assistance to Travelers* (IAMAT) which will provide valuable help in case you become ill while traveling.

On our recent cruise, I developed water on the knee from hiking on uneven ground in Borneo. The ship's physician gave me medicine and a knee bandage charging a good fee for his services. During the course of the long cruise, our medical tab came to over $100. Luckily I kept my bill, remembering our Trip Insurance policy covered accidents. A check to pay for our medical costs was welcome!

Find out if the excursions mentioned in the brochure will cost extra, and if so, how much more. Usually, sightseeing is included in tour plans, but sometimes it is merely available. On cruises, excursions are extra, but on freighters, they may be offered with compliments of the Line.

On our long cruise, a day's trip to the Taj Mahal by air was costly, as were five day trips into Kenya on a safari. The Yugoslavian Line treated the freighter passengers as guests paying for their hotel accommodations in Rijeka and a trip north to Lipica where the Lippazaner horses are trained.

It doesn't pay to wear expensive jewelry, not even the popular gold chains. A friend had hers ripped off her neck while walking along a dock. Crime is everywhere, and you are a target when you step off a luxury liner. Dress as conservatively as possible.

Many people dread the word, Customs, but if you have listed all your purchases on the declaration sheet and packed them in one suitcase, much of the frustration can be avoided.

A few years ago, my daughter, two grandchildren, and I took a ten day cruise to the Caribbean. We drove to Miami and parked our car on the dock. It was a cruise especially for children with masquerades and games.

As we prepared to leave the ship, a friendly passenger suggested we wait to clear customs after the crowd had left. We played cards in the lounge until he gave the signal for us to leave. Declaration slip in hand, we went down the ramp to find no one there. As we left the ship, I saw custom agents getting into their cars. No one came forward to take our declaration, so we went to our car and drove home.

Once going through customs, we were detained at the detection gate. One of the security guards motioned for me to step aside. A woman in uniform asked me to enter a little room where she frisked me, a mortifying experience. Harry and a guard were waiting for us. He held up my pocketbook. "Open it please," he ordered. It was then I realized what had triggered the alarm. My handbag was made like a small satchel and had a false bottom with a mirror where I kept cosmetics. This trip I had stored our magnetic scrabble set there. The squares had magnetic dots that held them to the board. I opened this explaining how convenient it was for travel. Harry shook his head, and the guide advised me to leave the set home after this. With tightened security now, this would have caused trouble even on a cruise ship.

Long range planning for a trip should include preparing yourself physically. This means daily exercise. Walking is what you do most on any trip whether it's a bus tour, cruise, or plane flights. All travel involves sightseeing, and one must be able to walk to explore important points of interest.

I have often felt sorry for someone who must stay on the bus while the rest of the tour departs because she is unable to walk. Even with an exercise program long before you depart, you may encounter more climbing than anywhere at home. Our first trip to London was so exciting that whenever we went anywhere by bus, I insisted the only place to sit was on the upper deck. From our seats on this high perch, we didn't miss anything on our trip from Bayswater to Picadilly. However, climbing up the steep steps proved my undoing. I developed severe back pains. Foolishly, I didn't heed the warning and kept on with strenuous sightseeing.

I was determined not to cut short our stay in Switzerland so, despite acute discomfort, continued our sightseeing. I was always the first to sit on any chair (they need more chairs on which to sit, especially in the art museums). I spent most of my days sitting at sidewalk cafés drinking coffee and sketching. Harry walked about and reported what he'd seen.

Muscle relaxing medicine helped, but what I needed was rest which I didn't get until I reached home.

As I have mentioned, it's rare a traveler doesn't experience an upset stomach usually caused by drinking water. On a cruise, it's best to take a morning tour and then return to the ship for lunch, especially in the third world countries. Now much has been discovered to eliminate seasickness. Before one leaves home, it is wise to consult your doctor about seasickness pills or a patch behind your ear. It's also smart to have pills to relieve dysentery from water and food contamination. Even with these aids, it is often impossible to avoid some discomfort.

A friend took a post in the Sudan and became very ill because he was not immune, as were the natives, to certain viruses. Wherever one goes, there is a risk of becoming ill, but this shouldn't discourage travel. How many people visit Mexico and, despite their precaution to eat only cooked fruit and vegetables and drink only boiled water, become sick for a short time. What pleasures and adventures would be missed if we were afraid to venture forth and take any chances!

Cruises are popular because of the varied entertainment and meals, but beware of overeating. Your new clothes will become too tight, and you won't feel your best. Sampling foods can be an adventure as long as you are careful.

Even though you may not be going out of the country soon, it is smart to keep your passport in order. It often takes four weeks for processing. Should you decide to take advantage of a last minute opportunity at a great discount, it would be disappointing to forego this chance because your passport isn't current. Finding out if you need a visa or special immunization shots is important, too.

Keep an open mind about the states or countries you'll be visiting. When we arrived in Morocco, I thought of the old musical, "The Desert Song" about a handsome Valentino type sheik who carries a captive white girl across the Sahara into the Atlas Mountains where his band of Riffs are hiding.

Everything the operetta depicted was true, the Riffs and the Atlas Mountains, except the only man good looking enough to be my hero turned out to be a local guide.

When our freighter docked too late for us to go to Dubrovnik in Yugoslavia, I was keenly disappointed. To my surprise, our bus took us to Kotor, a walled city our guide said was more interesting because the tourists hadn't found it. I hear Kotor is now being restored and will become a second attraction.

In Denmark, we were surprised to learn there is a vast area called Jutland with a large town, Arhus, a medieval city that equals any in Europe. And we had thought the only place worth seeing was Copenhagen!

If your time is limited, don't try to see everything on your first trip. When Americans first discovered Europe, there was a mad dash to see all the important cities in two weeks on the "Grand Tour." The movie, *"When It's Tuesday, You're in Belgium,"* featured a woman traveler completely confused about which country she was seeing. Imagine what little pleasure you would have if your trip was so hectic and so jammed with sightseeing that on your return, you couldn't remember many details about your trip, but only what it cost!

The traveler's attitude is important. Are you suspicious of foreigners? Do you look for a McDonald's or a sign "American food served here?" Are you friendly with everyone including the ship's crew and room steward?

However, it's wise to be wary of taxi drivers everywhere. In the U.S., meters protect the travelers, but abroad, the rule is when a taxi driver takes you from the station or airport, ask him to drive right up to your hotel, and have the doorman set the fare. He knows the right amount you should pay the driver for your ride.

Today we have expert assistants to help us make our travel plans. First, there is the travel agent, a much maligned person, for often it is thought she charges for her services when, in reality, she collects her commission from hotels and airlines for one's independent travel. There is a saying that one should choose his travel agent as carefully as his doctor or dentist. With one who is dedicated to serving you and being sure you will have the best wherever you might be going, it can be a very pleasant relationship.

Because of freighter travel where passage is booked through *Traveltips*, a freighter magazine which offers customer service, we have made our arrangements, cabin reservations, etc. without another agent. In Grand Circle Travel, they handle all bookings long distance out of New York, so that eliminates any other agent.

Elderhostel is much the same way. A catalogue is sent by Elderhostel six times a year divided into spring, summer, fall, and winter with additional supplements involving international programs. A variety is offered from one to three week periods where residential programs include twelve hundred institutions in fifty states, ten Canadian provinces, and forty foreign countries. Popular sites fill fast.

Your departure city should be one that is close and convenient for you to reach. New York is still the main port for travel to Europe, but Kennedy Airport has deteriorated so we now try to avoid using it. The last time we were there, the escalators were out of commission when we left for Scandinavia and were still out of service when we returned three months later!

No matter whether you sail, fly, or take a train, it pays to investigate your accomodations, even if it's only for a short time. Are they the best you can afford? I don't mean luxury hotels, because often a small family owned inn can give you better service, food, and a feeling of intimacy not available in hotels crowded with tourists.

Your travel agent sometimes can't find accommodations in off-beat places, because most of her business is with large tours, and there is more demand for more popular places. In 1970, we decided to explore the Virgin Islands and spent three weeks on St. Croix, St. Thomas, and St. John. We had no difficulty in finding rooms of our choice on the first two, but Vice President Humphrey and his entourage had taken over the vast Caneel Bay Resort on St. John. Our travel agent knew of no other place where we could stay. In my Fodor, I found Lille Maho, a small resort "perfect for a brief respite from city life." We knew this island was less developed than the others, but still we were not prepared, when our boat landed at Cruz Bay, for only a few cottages and just two cars to meet the passengers. One was an antique Lincoln, a touring model, that had fresh flowers in a vase on its hood, and a chauffeured driver who announced in a soft toned dialect that she was from Lille Maho and looking for the Lymans. She drove us up a steep hill and stopped at its summit, pointing below at the turquoise sea. We didn't see the small rowboat until she honked and a man beside it waved a flag.

"Why in the world is she signalling him?" Harry asked. I shook my head, wondering, too. Our driver continued down the road until she reached the beach and the small boat we'd seen from above. The sailor pushed out his craft from shore and we followed our driver's example of taking off our shoes, and followed her into the water. After she tossed our suitcases into the boat, we climbed in and were rowed around the bend. "You didn't tell me we had to reach this place by another boat", Harry whispered.

Our driver was waving to a man on the beach. He called, "Welcome to Lille Maho," as he began to unhitch two burros from a palm tree. Harry looked at me, shaking his head. What next? We climbed out of the boat into the shallow water and followed our luggage ashore. Our suitcases were strapped on the burros' backs, and we began a steep climb through the dense foliage. Halfway to the top, our small entourage stopped, and our bags were deposited on the porch of a little hut half hidden by flaming bougainvillea.

"This is yours," our guide, Marie, said. Dazed, we went into the cottage to find a huge double bed shrouded in mosquito netting. "It's just like Burma," Harry said. During World War II, he had fought under General Stilwell in the China-Burma-India theater. I managed to sit on the bed. It was comfortable enough.

"Your breakfast will be sent down every morning, but for lunch and dinner you will eat at the main house," Marie said. "You are the only guests."

What followed was an unforgettable week. Our host was an ex-Hollywood script writer and his wife was from one of the remaining Danish families. Bill's dream of writing a prize winning play or novel had not materialized and he had turned to drinking. He was the cook and the meals he created were delicious and imaginative. Freshly caught fish was broiled and served on wide plantain leaves with baked breadfruit and frangipani. Bill's conversation at dinner was brilliant, but when the dessert came, he retired to his bedroom. We could hear his snores as we drank our coffee on the veranda.

We had no transportation and neither Bill or Helene offered to drive us even to Cruz Bay. One day, the house boys drove us to town in the jeep. What an experience that was! We sat in the back seat and as the jeep careened around curves on the narrow road, the young men called to local girls. "Hi ya, baby," and "Luv ya, toots", rang out even when they drove into the prestigious Caneel Bay. It was a novelty to enter through the service entrance and greet the workers, instead of the guests. When we returned home, our travel agent shook her head after she heard of our adventure. "I was really worried about you," she confessed.

Tour guides deserve special note. On St. Thomas on the same vacation, antiquated busses were waiting on the dock to take us on an island tour. Some displayed outlandish banners on their sides. *"Heart Desire"*, *"Lover Boy"*, and *"Honey Bunch."* We chose

*"Lover Boy"* because the small driver had an infectious smile and fast lingo assuring us he would show us all the sights.

Little did we dream that this man in ragged blue jeans and gaudy shirt was a walking anthology of poetry! As he jerked the old bus into gear, he said "In Xanadu did Kubla Khan a stately pleasure dome decree - it was a miracle of rare device, a sunny pleasure dome with eaves of ice!" The temperature was ninety degrees, so it's a small wonder his thoughts were about ice. This bit of Coleridge was just a starter.

Soon he launched into his favorite as we left Charlotte Amalie (cha-cha town.) "Tell me not in mournful numbers life is but an empty dream! For the soul is dead that slumbers, and things are not what they seem."

Harry's face mirrored his amazement that this man should know Longfellow. "Bedspread" (that was actually his name) waxed eloquent. "Life is real! Life is earnest! And the grave is not the goal; dust thou art, to dust returnest, was not spoken of the soul." Harry joined him in "Lives of great men all remind us we can make our lives sublime. And departing, leave behind us footprints on the sands of time." We'll always remember "Bedspread" and his dreams.

We returned to St. Thomas in 1991 and found the

old busses gone. Open air jitneys take tourists about, giving photographers ample opportunity to film the local color. Charlotte Amalie is no longer a sleepy town. Sometimes as many as thirteen cruise ships call there in one day. They have berths along the new dock where many duty-free shops await the shoppers. We thought of Bedspread and his poetry.

Another kind of guide was in England. He was a big man who wore a beret jauntily over one eye. Amazingly he too recited poetry, this time Wordsworth. Every morning as we boarded the bus, he would say, "Let's chug along." As we rode through Cornwall and Devon, he would say, "My heart leaps up when I behold a rainbow in the sky. So it was when my life began, so it is now I am a man." The name, Cecil, seemed to suit him. During that week's bus trip, he revealed a knowledge of history and literature that was truly remarkable.

In Capetown, South Africa, our guide was a college professor, who was delighted that an American cruise line had docked there after such a long absence. The embargo and trade sanctions imposed by the U.S. on South Africa had taken their toll.

As we drove out of the city to Stellenbosch, Brian, our guide, explained how the vineyards had been developed and the wineries increased in volume and popularity. It was a surprise to most of us to find this part of the world very civilized and European.

Our guide in Mombasa, Kenya, was a large black man who was a Muslim, wearing white and a small fez-like cap. He waxed eloquent when he showed us hundreds of young black boys carving animals from teak and mahogany under a shelter of thatched canopies. He was so proud they didn't use a model or drawing to create realistic wildlife.

So many guides are helpful, and even when there is a language barrier, much of the information is understood. On a recent cruise, all our guides were graded from one to ten. That way, at the end of the trip, they can be rated and asked to serve again, or they can be rejected. Our guide in Norway did not talk very much but played Grieg's *Hall of the Mountain King*. This was worth a hundred words!

# 13

# HOW TO ADAPT TO FOREIGN CULTURE

*Unloading the fish, Agadir, Morocco, 1982.*

# HOW TO ADAPT TO FOREIGN CULTURE

Did you know ninety-five percent of the world is un-American?

We are so used to our own customs that we don't realize how different they are from other countries. In Germany, you should arrive on time, in Latin America, it's best to come late. We call people by their first names. In many cultures, that's rude.

One of the differences that has shocked me is the ladies' restroom. I finally managed how to ask where it was. *Donde esta el cuarto para damas?* (Spanish) *Ou sont les toilettes pour dames?* (French) When you finally find it, be prepared for a shock. In Yugoslavia, en route to Kotor, one of our passengers suffered from diarrhea. I got off the bus with her and went in the direction our guide pointed. An old woman attended what looked like an outhouse. She shook her head when we tried to go in, then took out a coin and pointed to it. We had no local money and no change. My tour friend said she couldn't go back to the bus. Desperate, I found a dime in my jacket, and shoved it into the woman's hand. At first I thought she would refuse it, but seeing the pain in my companion's face, she accepted it and opened the door. There was a hole in the dirt floor! The American went in and shut the door. I'll always remember the expression on her face.

A few months ago we were shopping at the Stanley Market in Hongkong. I had the urge to go to the restroom and finally was directed to a building in which there were a few cubicles, divided by half doors. There was a hole in the ground, and I found it very difficult to get in the right position. I wished I had been born a man.

I don't know why, but we all hate to use the word, "toilet." We prefer restroom, powder room, and comfort station instead. However, if we don't say "toilet", foreigners won't be able to help us. Except for Americans, women are held in low esteem, and I guess foreign restrooms confirm this.

The English are much like us though. Their loos are like our toilets except sometimes the plumbing looks like ours of the nineteenth century. While staying at the University of London a week in the Elderhostel program, we were lucky enough to have a private room and bath. The toilet had a chamber tank high above the seat, and when you flushed, there was a chain to pull. However, we had no luck yanking the chain. Harry, remembering how he used to prime a pump on his farm, went to the desk for a pitcher. Then he stood on the toilet seat and poured water into the tank. He instructed me when to pull, but try as we could, nothing happened. Later, I asked the couple next to us who had no problem flushing for advice. "You must hold the chain down for three seconds, then release it suddenly. "We tried that and it worked.

We Americans are very private people. We insist on being hidden when we relieve ourselves. In foreign countries, open urinals are on the street. In some countries, it's not unusual to see someone urinating beside the road.

Eating etiquette also can be very different. We like to have our silverware carefully placed on the table and to eat our meals in courses. How different it is in China where a large steaming bowl is brought in containing a chicken with its legs hanging over the rim, and guests are ready to attack it with their chopsticks. How do we prepare ourselves against culture shock? At first, a traveler can be fascinated by other customs, but this wears off if he stays very long. The best way is to learn more about the society and country you will be visiting. It helps to know simple greetings, like "Good Morning", and

"It's nice to be here." Learn how to say yes and no, and try to keep a low profile. If you smile and are friendly, the reception can be relaxed and warm.

A lot depends on what you wear. Women should never wear shorts in third world countries. To show bare legs is an offense to a Muslim. Arms and head should be covered in deference to his religion. Inconspicuous dress is always wise anywhere you travel.

Foreigners visiting in this country marvel that we eat corn on the cob. They feed their animals with it. Other foods are novelties like grits, pumpkin pie, and marshmallows. They eat their main meal at noon, as do our senior citizens and farming families. In business here, time is money, but many overseas companies like to socialize when they meet. Our cocktail hour is unique, and especially different is our custom of chilling our drinks with ice, a preference rarely found abroad. Fortune cookies are an American idea.

What has this to do with travel? Wherever you go, whether it's to another state or another country, customs and, especially foods, may be different. It's fun to enjoy something new.

When we were first married, we moved from Chicago to Macon, Georgia. It was a little hard to overcome the Civil War prejudice between northerners and southerners, but after a while, the townspeople realized we were acceptable even though we were "damn Yankees." We grew to like catfish, hominy, and black eyed peas. We also became more relaxed, not spending a lot of excess energy on some project, but taking more time visiting with our neighbors.

Another time we lived in New England, and being a midwesterner, I found our neighbors' reserve and what I thought was unfriendliness hard to bear. But after a while, I made friends and realized that they were just slow to respond. Many of them lived far apart on farms and were used to spending long periods alone without communicating with anyone.

When we moved back to the midwest, it was quite a change. We hadn't realized how easy it was to make friends there.

The far west is in marked contrast to the east. California sets the tone as you will see when you visit there. Styles and a way of life are relaxed and individual. On my first trip to San Francisco, we had dinner at 9 p.m., starting first with salad as the first course, a novelty for me.

When you travel about the U.S., you'll notice contrasts in local music. Taking a radio along when you're on a trip or using your car radio will help you adjust to Appalachian culture and Kentucky Blue Grass.

One of the best ways to prepare for a trip in the U.S. is to read a novel with background of that region, or one with authentic history. We especially liked the novel, *Sacajawea* by Anna Lee Waldo, when we followed the Lewis and Clark route to the northwest. Anyone coming to Florida would enjoy Margaret Rawlings' *Cross Creek.* William Faulkner captured the spirit of Mississippi in his novels. In the library, it's easy to find regional books, and these will increase your understanding of an area you plan to visit. Most of us associate Atlanta with *Gone With The Wind,* but the Margaret Mitchell's story is just as interesting in Anne Edwards' *Road To Tara.*

For anyone going to the Polynesian Islands, it's hard to beat James Michener's *Tales Of The South Pacific.*

Rudyard Kipling, Somerset Maugham, Ernest Hemingway all have written about places popular to visit.

In the U.S., we can wear mostly what we please except when restaurants or hotels request that men wear ties and jackets for dinner. Wherever you have accommodations, the hotel guide will let you know the proper dress. Sometimes dress is determined by the weather. In extreme heat and sun, you'll need hats and enough clothing to keep from becoming too sunburned.

In Moslem countries, clothes are important. Women should cover their arms and legs. When entering a mosque, shoes are removed, and heads are covered. I was told never to look a Moslem straight in the eye as this was an invitation to him. In fact, it's wise for American women to stay in a group while sightseeing abroad. Foreigners feel free to make advances, and it's wise to know defensive words like "no" in their language.

A business man we know often traveled to Japan. Once he gave a talk before a large audience there. Using the American custom of telling a joke before he launched into his subject, he found his audience received his humor with uproarious laughter. Later he spoke to the interpreter about it. The man shrugged. "I told them you would first tell a joke, and they should laugh. After that I started to translate your speech."

There are some local customs Americans often don't know. For example, you might insult a Brazilian by speaking Spanish to him; his language is Portuguese. If you have a chance to introduce yourself to a Chinese, Korean, or Japanese, it's important to hand him your business card.

It pays to take a refresher course on a language you may have learned in school. We both minored in French and found, although our accent is deplorable, we have managed to make ourselves understood in some foreign countries. In Morocco, a young security guard was eager to talk to us. His English was limited, but he managed to ask us to his home for tea. We carefully noted the time, 4 p.m., and returned from our sightseeing early to be ready for his arrival on the dock. We waited twenty-five minutes, and then thinking that we had misunderstood him, became involved with some activity on our ship. The next morning he met us with a "Where were you? Did you forget?" We explained we had waited at 4 p.m. Quatre heures. He shook his head. *"Quatre heures et demi."* Four-thirty. We tried to explain our mistake and disappointment. He had even polished his silver for the Americans coming to tea. We should have repeated the time to be sure we understood.

Another time in Paris, I asked the taxi driver to take me to the Eiffel Tower. He shook his head, *"Je ne sais pas."* (I don't know it.) I always carry a sketch pad, so I quickly drew a picture. *"Ah oui, le Eiffel Tour."* So much of French depends on the accent.

American travelers are handicapped by their lack of foreign language mastery. Only when we travel to other parts of the world, do we realize English is not spoken everywhere. Tour guides act as buffers with their fluidity in language. In fact, it's required of them, but this leaves Americans dependent on them for interpreting anything foreign.

Anxious to communicate in some way with local people, Harry and I often resort to gestures or use a sketch pad to convey an idea. A smile goes a long way to establish warmth between a foreigner and yourself.

Even in the U.S., our religions divide us, and as Protestants, we only know Christmas and Easter. The Catholics celebrate the Feast of the Immaculate Conception, and the Jews have Pentecost and Passover. When we travel abroad, we become more aware of these celebrations. Recently, we were in India and found the merchants in the shops were short tempered because they were fasting during the sacred month of Ramadan, most important to Islamic people. I should mention here that you should never photograph images of Buddha without permission. It's important to consider these religious festivals and customs when making travel plans.

Even though natives sometimes speak fluently, it is never spoken or understood in the same way it is at home. For instance, foreigners will use some of our expressions in the most comical ways. "Let me pick the worms from your nose" is their way of saying "Pick your brains." "Well, now the penguin has swung the other way" and "I smell a rat, and I intend to nip it in the bud," are other examples. And who was Sir Francis Drake? "He circumcised the world, using the world's largest clipper."

While visiting in Houston, an Arab drove up in a stretch limousine. He offered a guest, who greeted him, some wine. "Well, up yours," he toasted. When we say, "Out of sight, out of mind" some foreigners describe the man as an "invisible idiot." When Carter came to Poland, the headlines there read, "President Came Here To Grasp Our Secret Parts."

George Bernard Shaw says England and America are divided by a common language. Most of us are familiar with telly, fridge, and chemist's, but it's hard to remember a car hood is a bonnet, and the trunk, a boot. If you use the word "fanny", remember it's an X-rated word in England.

Once we were at the Tampa Airport, waiting for our plane to Miami, and then on to London. As usual, I wore a wide brimmed hat. This one I'd bought in Harrods', a London department store, the year before. While Harry stayed with our luggage, I made sure our tickets were in order and asked for seat assignments. The young man smiled at me. "How is everything over there in London?" Surprised, I murmured, "I hadn't heard of any trouble there." He continued to grin and said, "Milady, I've got a treat for you and your hubby." I watched him make out our seat assignments, wondering what he meant. It was only when he gave me an envelope and said, "We like to have you Brits over here," that I realized he thought I was British. Later we found on our flight to Miami, he had put us in First Class even though we had an Apex ticket. We enjoyed the deluxe meal with complimentary cocktails. Harry advised me to wear that hat often. I did and was amused in London to find a group of Girl Guides dressed exactly like me - navy skirt, white shirt, and the hat.

In our travels, we have found making an attempt to speak the language of the country we're visiting has been well received. Maybe we only can say hello - ("*Jambo*" in Kenya), "*Habla usted Ingles*?" ("Do you speak English?" in Spanish), "*No entiendo*" or "*je ne comprend pas*" (I don't understand), or "*Si, por favor*" (yes, please). In shopping, it helps to know "*Cuanto cuesta*? (How much is it?) or "*Esta caro*!" (It's too much!).

Even in our country, we have certain regional expressions like "fixin' to go", "throw myself down for a nap", "ayuh" (yes) and "go down the road a piece." It's very hard to understand the mountain people of Tennessee and conversation among Georgians and Mississippians. Out in Arkansas they have a way of speaking that is hard to follow. Natives of some states like Vermont don't say much, whereas those in Kentucky are known for their stories. Wherever you travel, you're bound to find language and customs different from yours at home.

That's why discovering another way of life is so interesting.

Greetings vary everywhere. The Japanese bow and don't like anyone touching them. In Latin America, hugs and cheek kisses are welcomed. We shake hands. In Europe, a kiss on both cheeks is customary.

Many people travel to shop. If you pack a collapsible bag in the bottom of your suitcase to carry home your souvenirs, and keep all your purchases in it, it will be easier to go through customs. Keep a list of what you buy, making note of what you paid in foreign currency and the equivalent in U.S. dollars. It's a good idea to check prices in your local stores before you go. A watch in Hongkong may not be such a bargain. Duty-free shops don't always offer a saving.

Sizes vary in different countries. Guide books have tables of clothing sizes, and it's handy to carry a card in your purse for reference. The one I have has sizes for Americans, Japanese, English, and Continentals. If you fall in love with an art object or antique, be sure you can get it out of the country. There are laws against the export of such items. In Africa, the sale of ivory is banned as are things made from elephant hair, or birds' feathers.

In public markets in third world countries, bargaining is the rule. Start at half the price offered and arrive at a price in between. This procedure made me uncomfortable, but the natives expect it. Personally, I liked the stores that had fixed prices. In India, the government emporiums have set prices.

It's always handy to have dollar bills in your wallet or purse. It came as a shock to find other countries' currencies so unstable that their paper money often has little value because of inflation. It made us realize how lucky we are to have money that does not lose its value over a period of a few days.

Even our transportation can be so different. The jeepneys, old World War II jeeps, are popular in Manila, and in Bangkok, the popular way of getting places is the tuk tuk. In Mombasa, the dhow sails up the rivers, and in Hongkong, sampans and water taxis take you everywhere.

England is known for its double decker busses, and Japan for its crack bullet trains. Our American cars have a different character abroad, like the Fords in Europe. However we travel, it's an adventure. Robert Louis Stevenson says it aptly, "For my part, I travel not to go anywhere, but to go. I travel for travel's sake. The great affair is to move."

# 14

# SEEING THE WORLD

*The Maldives, Panama Canal, Tampico, Mexico, Women in Malaysia, 1991.*

# SEEING THE WORLD

Many people dream of going around the world, but few do. We are one of the lucky couples who, as a celebration of our 50th anniversary, sailed for 106 days on the same ship encircling the globe. Fort Lauderdale to Fort Lauderdale, stopping at thirty-one ports of call and following the route of Capt. James Cook through the Polynesian Islands to Australia.

Anyone who has heard we had taken such a voyage asks, "Wasn't that too long to stay on a ship? Didn't you get bored? Didn't you gain weight?" Some even asked, "How could you afford such a trip? How did you pay your bills and what about the income tax?"

It was hard to describe our life at sea, the fascinating ports of call, the lecturers from various universities who knew so much about the history, geography, and political background of Polynesia, Asia, Africa, and South America. Our charts were similar to those of Captain James Cook, who, in turn, was influenced by Marco Polo and Magellan.

Sailing westward encircling the globe, across thousands of miles of ocean, the very thought stretches the imagination. We've tried to tell our friends about our busy life aboard our ship, learning something new from our captain who talked with us every morning explaining why we lost a day, how he rescued a shipwrecked crew in the Java Sea, or what weather conditions to expect in that part of the world.

Our first port was Williamsted, Curaçao in the Dutch Antilles. Because the glare of the tropical sun on white buildings blinded the governor, he ordered the residents to paint their houses yellow, blue, and pink. These with red tiled roofs present a colorful picture. Once a slave trading island, Curaçao has become prosperous because of the Royal Dutch Shell refinery that processes Venezuelan oil there.

Sailing though the Panama Canal's locks, a miracle of engineering, from the Atlantic to the Pacific, is an exciting experience and the only time our captain gave complete control to canal pilots. An ever changing landscape of great beauty passed by as we made the transit.

Two Mexican resorts were next on our itinerary, Acapulco and Cabo San Lucas. Our covered tender took us ashore and it wasn't long before we were watching the famous cliff divers. It's remarkable there have been few fatalities in the dive from three hundred feet to a small channel below. In contrast to Acapulco, Cabo San Lucas is not as yet developed. They use old busses called *truks* for island tours. Some of us wished we had time to catch marlin in this well known fishing village. The dramatic rock formations and endless beaches invited us to stay longer.

The end of our cruise's first segment was Los Angeles. There many left the ship, and new passengers joined us for the voyage across the Pacific.

As we sailed westward across what seemed an unlimited stretch of sea, James Michener's *Tales Of The South Pacific* came to mind. "I wish I could tell you about the South Pacific. The way it actually was. The endless ocean, the infinite specks of coral we called islands. Coconut palms nodding gracefully toward the ocean. Reefs upon which waves broke into spray, and inner lagoons, lovely beyond description, the sweating jungle, the full moon rising behind the volcanoes."

Bora Bora, our next port of call, was the setting for Michener's *South Pacific* (*Here am I, your special island.*) One hundred fifty miles northwest of Tahiti,

Bora Bora is a part of the Society Islands and French Polynesia. As our glass bottom boat cut through the turquoise water near the white beach, and went over the coral reef, exotic fish swam beneath us - Parrotfish, Manta Ray, Wrasse, Butterfly, and Goatfish darted among the giant clam shells.

A band of native musicians played for us on the dock. Tourists are supposed to have influenced this island more than World War II when it was a supply base for the Solomon Islands campaign. A view from the water of the rugged volcanic peaks, and white beaches is better than taking a land tour through the areas where poor people live. Bora Bora is not as prosperous as the guide book says.

Nearby is Tahiti, an island that inspired Robert Lewis Stevenson, Rupert Brooke, and Gauguin. It is larger than Bora Bora and attracts more interest. *Mutiny On The Bounty* was researched here by Nordhoff and Hall, and when Marlon Brando played in the film, he decided to buy a nearby island. The capital, Papeete, is crowded and nowhere on our three hour tour did we see the girls with long hair and printed skirts depicted in Gauguin's paintings. To our dismay, our guide allowed a longer time at the Hyatt Regency than at the archeological museum. There a Tahitian man appeared naked, except for a loin cloth, his curly long hair pinned to one side with flowers. Our guide introduced him as a cousin, the tourist sensation of Moorea, where he climbs coconut palms as an attraction!

As we sailed away, we thought again of Gauguin who immortalized Tahitians depicting their simple lives. A museum bears his name, but the paintings are elsewhere in galleries abroad. The sad history of the whalers killing the natives because they were heathens, and the missionaries bringing disease and making them wear heavy clothes is hard to forget.

Native musicians on the dock greeted us in Raratonga. Here lovely girls welcomed us with leis of frangipani as we boarded our bus. It is believed the first Europeans to set forth on this Cook Island was Fletcher Christian and his mutineers from the *Bounty* who introduced the first citrus seeds.

What a contrast between French Polynesia and Raratonga, a protectorate of New Zealand, which sends it produce when it's wintertime. These handsome people are joyous as they perform their native dances. The island is very clean with well tended houses and lawns. There is an outrigger yacht club, and an artist lives there, calling himself a modern Gauguin.

Our next stop was at the last Polynesian kingdom in the world, Tonga. Unlike the other islands, there are no mountains here. Its capital, Nuka' Alofa, is on a deep blue lagoon. A police band in snappy black uniforms welcomed us. The rainy day lent a depressing note to the poverty we found there despite the fact the king and his family live well and spend several months in England. Here, "Fat is Beautiful." The king sets the fashion by weighing four hundred pounds, and his wife is almost as big. Some of the buxom passengers on our ship were delighted to find natives larger than they.

Tonga exports copra from which coconut oil is extracted. Small boys climbed the very tall palms to cut down the coconuts. Tapioca is another crop.

On our way back to the ship, we met some girls who had large bags attached to their waists. They told us they were Methodists, and the bags were symbols of mourning. Their father had died. As the gangway was lifted, strains of *Auf Weidersehen* came from the police band. As our ship moved away, the captain sounded the ship's horn, a long blast; then the police band imitated it to everyone's delight.

The New Hebrides, which is now called Vanuatu, was our next port of call. This is a Melanesian Island, quite different from the Polynesian, because the natives are of darker skin and are reminders of the slave trade. In the early days, there was "blackbirding", a practice in which natives were captured and taken to work as slaves in Queensland and Fiji. As a result, the first missionary, Rev. John Williams, was murdered.

Our guide told of their custom of extracting the front tooth of a girl to show she was married. Now this is no longer done.

World visitors come to see a young boy jump from the tower. When Queen Elizabeth visited a few years ago, it was not the month in which the jump was made (April and May), but a native agreed to perform for the royal party. Unfortunately, he had not trained like the others who start jumping at two; he snapped his neck and died.

Since Vanuatu has become independent, everyone, including those on the outer islands, work. Their shops are modern, the people cheerful.

We were flying all our nautical flags as we sailed into Cairns, Australia. From our top deck overlooking the ship's bow, we saw small islands dark against a mountain range reminiscent of a Japanese painting.

After so many small islands, reaching a continent was exciting.

It was very hot, ninety-five degrees, and humid after six days of rain. It was the monsoon season. Cairns is a small city with a museum exhibiting pictures of aborigines. Capt. Cook went aground north of Cairns and later took possession of the entire east coast for Britain. With hundreds of men, mostly Chinese, a scenic railway was cut through the virgin forest to Kuranda.

Homes are on stilts because of the high tides and hot climate. An art gallery depicted Australians in the Outback. One could feel the dust, heat, and loneliness.

We heard the Australians take as much pride in tracing their convict ancestry, as we do our forefathers who came over on the Mayflower.

The next day we visited the Great Barrier Reef. There are 2600 individual reefs and about 300 islands, the largest complex of coral reefs in the world.

A giant aluminum jet-propelled catamaran, *Quicksilver,* transported us to the reef at 35 mph. In a short time, we arrived at the landing platform where some prepared to snorkel, and others to board the submersible boat to view the fish. I was on the latter and found windows on both sides to view the spectacular staghorn coral and tropical fish. Harry snorkeled and found the experience exhilarating. Yellowtail, Bonita, and Sea Bass swam among the brain coral and could be seen also from the seaquarium attached to the platform. This carefully protected habitat is vulnerable. The coral is being eaten by the crown-of-thorns starfish.

The next port held many memories for World War II servicemen aboard. Manila was the scene of Japanese occupation for three years. The gaily decorated jeepneys evolved from jeeps left at the end of the war, and is used generally for transportation. Another reminder of the war was Fort Santiago which was almost destroyed by bombs. It is there that hundreds of Filipinos and American prisoners were kept in dungeons to be drowned when the tide came in.

Another scene of the war was Corregidor, twenty-six miles from Manila. This rock fortress was where the Filipino president, Quezon, took refuge, and later General MacArthur returned to liberate it. Now only ruins and a few artillery pieces remain. We were impressed by the Pacific War Memorial, commemorating all the soldiers, Filipino and American, who died in this theater of the war.

When our ship arrived in Hongkong, our next port of call, it had completed the second segment of our voyage. From Los Angeles to Hongkong, we had sailed 11,026 nautical miles - 12,679 statute miles, and spent 33 days at sea.

Our ship docked at the Ocean Terminal next to the Queen Elizabeth 2, and suddenly the sounds and smells of the Orient assailed us. The premier city of Asia, Hongkong lives up to its reputation of being glamorous, for even in the early morning, the Star Ferry plies back and forth between Kowloon and Hongkong Island against a backdrop of eight mountains that ring the bay. One is transported into a Chinese world of contrasts, elegant homes on the summits looking down on shacks. Everyone works, and the vast city is very clean.

We rode in a covered water taxi to Aberdeen, home of the boat people. Our sampan darted between junks where large families live. Our guide said if one had money, he would own two junks, one for fishing, the other for living.

Riding the tram up Victoria Peak gave us a magnificent view of the harbor, and sky scrapers. The city stretches out for miles. At Repulse Bay, we felt the real Orient: the strong incense burning before the Buddhist temples, the gold Buddhas themselves, seated impassively looking over the visitors, the life-size statues of white rams (this was the Chinese year of the Ram.) At this lookout the Celestial Lion sculpture was unveiled by British Commander, Sir Richard Ward, in 1979.

At night the city comes alive with a blaze of lighted billboards that surpass Time Square's. Our Chinese junk took us out to see the sun setting behind the mountains.

Since we had three days in Hongkong, there was time to explore on our own. A ride from Kowloon to the Island on the Star Ferry proved interesting once we had found the booth to change our money. Mostly Chinese sat around us, chatting in Mandarin, Harry said. Only a few rickshaws, which we had expected to see everywhere, were waiting at the ferry terminal. A double decker English bus took us to the famous Stanley Market. As usual, we preferred the view from the top deck, but it proved a rough ride. The market was colorful, and to our relief, the prices were fixed. The smell of pungent food, cooking in woks along the street, permeated the air.

Shopping is synonymous with Hongkong. An expert had recommended tailors, and many passengers took advantage of the chance to have custom made suits and dresses. One man told of an order he had given to have his initials on his right pocket. When it arrived, the words "right pocket" were embroidered next to the initials. Pan Am pearls, found in shops on Nathan Road, were considered good buys and bought by some passengers.

A formal dinner was held that night for the passengers taking the full voyage, ninety of us. It was held in the new Grand Hyatt, an elegant hotel with black marble columns, polished floors, high ceilings, and beautiful Chinese rugs.

Cocktails were served on the mezzanine, and dinner in the Grand Ballroom. The orchestra was good, but the dance floor was very slippery.

The Ocean Terminal, where our ship was berthed, had many shops and articles of every description.

Nearby was the Cultural Center on the Bay. It cost billions of dollars, but the natives dislike the architecture, because there is little Chinese decor in its facade. However, the concert hall and large auditorium are magnificent. This was their off season, so there was no attraction offered.

In the evening, we sailed away to the strains of our Dixieland band, sipping champagne while we watched the twinkling lights of the city fade away.

The third segment of our trip was called "Passage to the Orient" and covered eleven days from Hongkong to Kota Kinabula, East Malaysia, to Bangkok, then on to Singapore. The total distance traveled was 1,050 nautical miles, or 1298 statute miles.

Kota Kinabalu is the capital of Sabah, North Borneo. Sailors surviving storms in the South China Sea called it "Land below the Wind." The most spectacular feature though is above the wind, the majestic Mount Kinabalu, the highest peak in Malaysia. Our guide told us that only fifty years ago, young men proved their virility by beheading someone. That's why there are so few men. Cannibalism was prevalent, too. According to her, women do all the heavy work and receive little more than a kick for their efforts. At one stop, we saw women working in a construction crew, with bare feet and dressed in tattered skirts.

Many are Moslems and have four or more wives. Few natives smiled.

The national forest had trails that were most difficult to follow, because they were so rocky and precipitous. At the village of Tamparuli, there was a foot bridge that spanned a wide, muddy river. I followed Harry, who wanted to photograph it, and found others behind me urging me on, until I was actually on the bridge, held up by the guide and clinging to the ropes on either side. With so many people crossing it, the bridge began to swing alarmingly. Always afraid of heights, I was terrified, because it was necessary to look down to avoid stepping into the holes made by missing slats. In the middle of the bridge, I paused to look below at the scene of water buffalo swimming and native women washing clothes on rocks; an experience I will never repeat.

Our next port of call had been long anticipated - Thailand, the most exotic country in Asia. This small country is unique because it was never colonized by a European power.

Our ship docked at Pattaya, and from there a bus took us on a three hour trip to Bangkok, where we made plans to spend the night at the Bangkok Regent, in order to see the floating markets on the quongs (canals) the next day.

Our first introduction to Thai architecture was at Wat Trimitr, a temple. Near it is a chapel that houses the eight century old Golden Buddha made of seven and a half tons of solid gold! Two hundred years ago this golden figure was covered by plaster when the Burmese invaded the country and was discovered by accident only several years ago.

This was our first night away from our ship. Our room at the Bangkok Regent delighted us with its spaciousness and Oriental decor — the Thai silk panel over our beds, kimonos and slippers in the bathroom along with various soaps and perfumes. As soon as we began unpacking, a Thai attendant arrived with a tray of tea and cookies. She knelt down beside the low coffee table and filled our cups smiling and saying, "Welcome".

The luncheons at the Regent were a disappointment, though. Every dish was so hot, I couldn't eat anything except the fruits and cake.

Afterwards, we visited the Grand Palace. The gates were guarded by ferocious lion sculptures, and within the whitewashed walls were government and religious buildings with ornate designs in gold. The sculptures of dancing Thai figures at the base of one temple were unforgettable. All the roof designs pointed to heaven. Adding to the Buddha mysticism were monks in loose flowing orange robes and closely shaved heads, standing in groups talking or resting beneath the banyan trees. Since our return, we have read of the Buddhist Eightfold Path, consisting of Right Views: Resolve, Speech,

Action, Livelihood, Effort, Mindfulness, Aspiration and Concentration.

The evening dinner at the Sawasdee Restaurant proved delicious. We sat at low tables, but since there was a recess in which to extend our legs, we did not have to assume a crosslegged position. Five different covered bowls contained hot dishes of rice, chicken curry, and sweet and sour vegetables.

On the stage, Thai dancers performed. The tall, slim girls gestured with long fingers bent back, and the men put down each foot with emphasis. The Thai music seemed off key and like nothing we had ever heard before. The costumes completely covered their figures and must have made them very uncomfortable in the heat.

Early the next morning, our bus took us to the Chao Phya River where we boarded flat, long boats for our trip to the quongs (canals) that branched off through densely populated areas of the city. The famous Floating Market consists of hundreds of small boats. Their vendors vie with each other selling produce and hats, which most of us bought, trying them on as our boat slipped along and then paying for them, the most difficult feat of all. Once there was a traffic jam and the only way we could climb ashore to buy something on the dock was to step from boat to boat. I managed to find a Thai scarf. Even buying some Thai silk that afternoon proved hazardous because our tuk-tuk, a small three wheeled vehicle, used as a taxi, had great difficulty finding its way through thousands of similar tuk-tuks and motorcycles.

Singapore was one place we had always wanted to visit. Conrad's novel, *Lord Jim* and Somerset Maughams' short stories had this exotic city for their background. Once named Singapura, "Lion City" because a visiting prince saw a lion here, this is the wealthiest nation in Southeast Asia. The majority are Chinese (76% with 15% Malay, and 7% Indian.)

The city was only a fifteen minute drive from our dock and our first stop was at the National Museum where tableaux with life size models of natives dressed the way they lived were exhibited: a typical wedding ceremony, a temple with people praying, and a social visit. A brightly painted lion-fish, often used in ceremonial dances, was also displayed.

The heart of the city is Chinatown. There a very old Chinese house is open to visitors. In front of it, in celebration of their New Year, were painted idols consecrated by burning incense. The house itself was built around a courtyard, living quarters on one side, animals sheltered on the other, and the shrine in the central section.

A drive up Mt. Faber was worthwhile because of the view of the city with gold domes of its temples and mosques gleaming in the sun was spectacular.

Another point of interest was the Botanical Garden with its myriads of orchids and other exotic plants.

No one visits Singapore without stopping at the famous Raffles Hotel, but since the war, it had badly deteriorated and is now being restored. We did have the famous Singapore Sling made of gin and lime juice at the Dynasty Hotel where the three story lobby is in deep, rich red, the Chinese color for good fortune.

The night before, our ship had hosted Malay dancers. One number featured the Lion-fish brought to life by two acrobats. When it rose on its hind legs, one man jumped upon the shoulders of the other.

We continued to be impressed with Malaysia. No one had said much about Kuala Lumpur, so it was a surprise to find this city not only as clean as Singapore, but even more beautiful. Our guide was one of the best and pointed out the rubber plantations along the way, stopping the bus to show us sap coming from the trees, the kernel that comes from the coco bean and black seed of an oil palm used to make cosmetics and medicine.

Malyasia's National Museum emphasized Malay folk traditions. One exhibit explains "waylang kulit", shadow plays performed with puppets cut from leather and manipulated with sticks. A simple light casts the figures on the screen as the story teller creates magic about folk legends.

The famous Blue Mosque is similar, I hear, to the one in Istanbul. The blue marble dome, surrounded by its five minarets and landscaped park, is impressive. Not long ago, muezzins had to climb the spiral staircases of these minarets five times a day to call Muslims to prayer, but now loud speakers and microphones in many mosques eliminate the need for the climb.

Half Malay and half Chinese, Kuala Lumpur is one of Asia's fastest growing cities. The Railway Station is a gem of architecture - part Islam, part Gothic. Behind the National Museum is the transportation shed with every transport used in the country: the Malacca bullock cart, the pedaled trishaw still used in Penang, and lastly, the symbol of Malaysian pride, the car, Proton Saga.

Now begins the fourth segment of our cruise, Singapore to Capetown, South Africa. It will take twenty-one days and we will sail 7,235 nautical miles/8,322 statute miles.

Nothing prepared us for the culture shock felt when we stepped onto the docks of Madras, India. Our foreheads were painted with red dots, symbols of good fortune, and crowds surrounded us: vendors, beggars (there were children among them), and tailors trying to take our measurements for clothes. My Oriental outfit bought in Florida and worn because it was cotton and cool was immediately pointed at, and several said, "Punjab". Someone later told me that was a province in northern India. With difficulty, we managed to board our bus for the morning tour.

It was very hot and dusty, and everything looked run down. A passenger who had been there when the British were in charge said nothing had been painted - the busses, the cars, the houses. Cows wandered about and stopped traffic. Hordes of pedestrians made it difficult to move. There were no sidewalks, and some men were sleeping beside the road. One woman was cutting her child's hair.

The one bright feature were the women. Even though children were often slung over their backs or carried on their hips, they moved gracefully in their loose flowing saris.

The neo-Gothic Cathedral of San Thomé stood out in marked contrast. This was the church of the apostle, St. Thomas, who came there shortly after the crucifixion to spread the gospel and was martyred. To our surprise, we learned fifteen hundred Hindus come there to worship every Sunday.

In the heart of the city was a handsomely carved shrine and sculpture depicting an Indian fairy tale. Against this backdrop, were stands with watermelon, and sacred cows nearby eating the rinds. Everywhere there were Hindus. The very old busses were packed with people of all ages.

The begging children followed us everywhere and often a cripple would stretch out a hand in our direction. A young boy crawling on the ground was a pitiful sight.

There are cottage industry shops, and in one we found hand embroidered skirts and blouses. The material for saris was so colorful, I bought one to wear for Sari Night that evening on the ship. There was a diagram included to show how to drape it.

Several times we had a chance to use the greeting, *Nama Stay*, pressing our palms together and bowing slightly. This was quickly returned with a smile.

That afternoon, the tour into the countryside proved to be hazardous. The narrow bumpy road could hardly accommodate two busses passing. Every car honked continually to drive people off the road. Luckily, the cows moved out of the way, too. I heard that if you hit a cow, it's worse than if you murder someone.

Our destination was Mahalaipuram, the site of magnificent sculptures - a life size elephant, bull, and lions, carved in granite. A bas-relief of a women milking her cow and other scenes of daily life were described by Marco Polo in 1292. Hindu mythology was depicted in cave temples.

How relieved we were to arrive safely at our ship! It was a miracle we hadn't been involved in an accident.

That night, Indian entertainers came aboard. They did not appear on the stage when our director announced them, and after he brought them out, they carried suitcases with their instruments. Slowly, a drum and keyboard with bellows emerged, and a dancer began her performance using gestures we later learned imitated that of a cobra. It was easy to see in the next dance that she portrayed a peacock as she fastened feathers to her belt. Another performer was to have narrated the dance, but didn't. The sing song voice and monotonous music caused much of the audience to leave early.

We came away feeling India's population was out of control and their lives had lost a great deal since the British left.

Three days sailing brought us to the Maldives, comprised of two thousand islands below the southern tip of India. This is the smallest country in south Asia. Malé, the only town and capital, was surprisingly clean with wide, brick streets, sidewalks, and substantial homes. The golden dome of the mosque and minaret could be seen long before we were near enough to anchor. Later we learned these had been built recently with Arab money. The people are Islamic. It was hot, but sitting under a tree near the mosque, I found the sea breeze refreshing and decided to paint a watercolor. Soon, I had the usual audience of children. One boy who spoke excellent English, told me his mother was very cross when he didn't go to prayer five times a day. His family's shop was nearby, and I went there to buy a shirt.

Malé was once the haven for criminals and social outcasts. Our ship anchored in the harbor when the captain, much to his annoyance, received word to move. There was surveillance of a distant island, and we interfered with their view. The passengers surmised there might still be drug running activity.

I met a lady on my way to the mosque. She had bicycled down from her home on the hill when our ship sailed into the bay. She turned out to be an Australian who had moved, with her family, from Tonga two years ago. She described her life as stressful. Their small shop had fallen on bad times because of lack of tourists.

I walked on the shaded side of the street (this city is four degrees above the equator) past a building that had a *Welcome* sign in front. It turned out to be a girls' school for teenagers. The principal, a charming black woman, was educated in England.

That afternoon, the ship's personnel had planned a picnic on a nearby deserted island. It was more like a luau. There were barbecue pits over which were roasted all kinds of fish and beef. In addition to fruits and desserts galore, there was a stand serving rum punch and beer. As we ate, a band played.

The beach was similar to ours in Florida, but the water was a light blue, and the current very strong. Many of us started swimming beyond the picnic spot and then floated down.

It was such an enchanting place we stayed until the last tender left.

Three days later we arrived at Mahé Island, the largest of Seychelles. Victoria, its capital, is one of the world's smallest capitals. The only reminders of its colonial past are the courthouse and postoffice. The island gained its independence from England in 1976. Curious to see the inside of the courthouse, which I thought might be a museum, I found myself in a room where court was in session. Behind a high desk was a black judge with gold rimmed glasses and a wig. Beside him was a light-colored girl who acted as interpreter of the native dialect. Before the bench stood a young woman and to the right a black man with a rakish moustache. The plaintiff was asking for child support, and the man kept saying, "But Judge, I have no money!" The judge,who spoke in British English, had little sympathy for him, suggesting he get a loan or borrow. At that moment, one of the officers from our ship opened the door and beckoned to me. As we returned to the ship, someone pointed out an island off shore used for anyone breaking the law. No wonder there was such order.

Three days later we arrived in Mombasa, Kenya. From here there were several excursions offered: a safari to Tsavo East National Park, hot air ballooning, Shimbo Hills Safari, and an air safari to Amboseli. We were content to explore Mombasa, our first African city. The entrance of the city had sheet metal elephant tusks twenty feet high that formed a double arch over the road.

The black people were different from any we'd seen - very tall, thin, and holding themselves proudly erect. The women dressed in loose, flowing dresses of bright design and carried baskets on their heads. These we saw at close hand in the market place where a few tourists roamed about, unnoticed by the natives. Some of the Muslim women were robed in black, their heads covered by chador that framed their lovely eyes.

The highlight of our visit was a handicraft center where hundreds of young black men sat under low thatched roofs carving animals from teak and mahogany. Having carved in wood myself, I was extremely interested in the vast workshop. All spoke English, but conversed among themselves in Swahili. They used no drawings or models to create various wild animals in all sizes. Rhinos, elephants, and giraffes were so life-like it was hard to imagine these had been made from memory. We bought a teak elephant and two giraffes of mahogany.

Everyone we met was friendly and smiled as we greeted them with *Jambo*. One of our passengers reported seeing a giant dhow in the river, jammed with people that were said to be refugees from Somaliland seeking refuge in Kenya.

Not many travelers have the chance to arrive in Mombasa by ship. Winston Churchill described the port, "The gate of Africa...the outlet of all the trade of all the countries that lap the Albert and Victorian Lakes and the headwaters of the Nile." It has a history that stretches back two thousand years. Settled first by the Arabs, then occupied by the Persians, Mombasa was discovered by the Portuguese explorer, Vasco da Gama, and then they, in turn, were driven out in 1725 by the Arabs. The old Fort Jesus was the scene of many battles and is over four hundred years old.

In the afternoon, I sat on the veranda of the Castle Hotel watching Arabs, Persians, Africans, and blacks walking by intent on their daily shopping for food. The man who brought me a cold drink carried on a rapid fire conversation with another. Their language was Swahili, a musical sing-song phrasing that was most pleasant.

Four days later we arrived in Durban, the "Riviera" of east Africa. It was a surprise to find this modern city with beautiful parks and colleges. There are supposed to be more Indians living here than any other place outside of India. As a result, our first stop was a spice market run for and by Indians. It was in a large building with many booths. There were displays of ivory and animal furs (banned in the U.S.), and a quantity of animal hides that were bought by some tourists. Articles of every description were sold here, and the atmosphere of incense, spices, and body odors from hordes of shoppers permeated the air.

Our next stop was at the Botanical Garden which proved to be outstanding in its display of roses and an aviary of native birds in large cages. The Crested Crane and the various kinds of Cocatiels were unusual. Tea and scones were served in a park restaurant.

We were surprised to see very few blacks, and none in native garb as in Mombasa. However, that afternoon we traveled to the vast Rift Valley where we met natives in the Phe-Zulu tribal Kraal. Enroute we passed the wealthy suburb, Kloof, meaning a deep ravine in Africaner. At a bazaar, we saw the first Zulu women, standing beside the road. They were bare breasted, a sign of virginity. Later, a Zulu settlement with beehive huts seemed set up for tourists. The natives were a pathetic group dancing and kicking unlike anything we had imagined. A Zulu woman told us that most of the Zulu Nation (what was left of a once proud people) now live in concrete houses.

Dredging of the harbor had made this port the outlet for the most cargo in South Africa. The beach with its surf has also drawn sports enthusiasts. Natal University, with its vast campus, has students from all over the world.

Two days later, the sight we'd been waiting to see appeared on our horizon. Table Mountain! The high cliffs rising from the sea with the flat top that gave the mountains its name could be seen for miles. As we approached we saw the Cape of Good Hope, where so many ships have foundered on the rocks. Our captain rounded the peninsula, pointing out as he did so, the Twelve Apostle peaks. The day was bright and sunny as the pilot boat approached, along with a fire boat that was shooting streams of water into the air as the passengers aboard cheered their welcome. Other small boats came too, tooting and adding to the celebration. By the time we reached the dock, everyone was on deck to watch the ceremony of a lavender Rolls Royce pulling up to our gangway. From it stepped the mayor of the city. Later he came aboard to present the captain with the keys to Capetown. The band on the pier played *Hello Dolly*, and a marching band led by baton twirlers paraded up and down. What a reception!

A red carpet was rolled out and pretty girls in colonial costume lined up on the runway to greet us as we stepped from the ship. Clearly, our government's sanctions, enforced because of the apartheid policy in South Africa, had isolated this country. Ours was the first major cruise ship to arrive in a long time.

So much has been written about the Bushmen that dwelled here originally that a visit to the museum seemed in order. There these aboriginals were depicted in life-size images in their native environment. To make these faithful reproductions, one of the few Bushmen left was covered with plaster with a few holes so he could breathe - and the casts made. The exhibit reminded us of Malvina Hoffman's bronze sculpture of Africans in the Chicago Field Museum. Sadly the Bushmen were treated as heathens by the missionaries, and pagans by civilized men and as such, were persecuted and killed. Only a few remain.

A cable car took us to the top of Table Mountain from which we could see for miles, and realize how wild the country still is. No wonder the Dutch East India company wanted to keep this area to themselves as a food supply line for their sailors. It is understandable that colonization was slow because of this monopoly. The Dutch were only interested in trade, and did not supply education or women needed to further the population here.

That night, a trip was planned for us to drive up

Signal Mountain in order to see the city and Table Mountain in the moonlight. To our delight, we found the mountain itself had been illuminated, so that its grooves were in dark contrast with the rocky escarpment. The entire city lay below us with thousands of twinkling lights. Another treat was a stop at a lookout point where champagne and cakes were served as refreshment.

The next day was our excursion to Stellenbosch, the oldest settlement, next to Capetown, in South Africa. This village reminded us of Williamsburg with its museum type white Cape Dutch houses. Their furnishings were of the best - delicate carved chests, and furniture of the colonial period in the finest mahogany. The Burgher House had a thatched roof and a stone wall around it. As it was very warm, a young Africaner security guard let me share the shade of his umbrella.

We left the town and drove a few miles east to the Neethlingshof Estate noted for its beauty and wines. A long avenue of stately trees led us to the mansion where we ate a delicious lunch. Before this, however, we were shown how wine was made, how the grapes are pressed and later the juice put in oak barrels to age. As it was a hot day, the cellar where we tasted various wines was refreshingly cool.

We sailed away at 8 p.m. to the music of our band on board. To our surprise, hundreds of people crowded onto the dock to wave goodbye. We threw streamers down to them, exhilarated by all the attention. No doubt the headlines in the Capetown newspaper, *The Argus,* had brought out the local residents. *World's Top Cruise Ship in Table Bay.* It describes Capetown as tourist hungry and us as super-rich travelers.

It was an unforgettable visit, and so unlike what we had pictured. The remarkable part is Capetown seemed totally European. We saw only a few blacks, but many Cape Coloured, a mixture of Hottentots and Europeans marrying with their Indian and black slaves. Then there are British, and Boers, or Africaners. It seemed more like Paris or London than a city at the tip of Africa.

After leaving South Africa, our ship began its longest voyage between continents, eleven days between Capetown and Buenos Aires.

The Atlantic Ocean is smaller than the Pacific, but receives four times as much drainage, because such rivers as the Mississippi, Amazon, and Congo flow into it.

The wind systems of the North and South Atlantic are similar, except that in the north the wind blows clockwise around an area of high pressure, and in the south it moves counter-clockwise around a similar area. Off the Cape of Good Hope, the roaring forties begin: extremely high winds and waves that exist because no islands or continents break up the build-up of water over thousands of miles. Here, the winds are westerly and blow without hinderance clear around the world.

That is why most of our seasoned travelers aboard expected rough sailing, and they were right. Soon waves assumed alarming heights, and the wind was so strong that for several days, no one could walk out on deck. Since our ship was new and had stabilizers, it did not roll or pitch much. Nevertheless, there was enough action to keep some people in their cabins.

Everyone hoped our long sea voyage would be broken by visiting a remote Atlantic island, Tristan da Cunha. It belongs to Great Britain and is 1,500 miles east of South Africa. One hundred and ninety-eight inhabit this island, where they grow potatoes. The sale of da Cunha postage stamps contributes to their income.

Some of our stamp collectors were looking forward to our visit, but, alas, the seas were too rough. Through binoculars we saw the people waiting on the shore beside their display stands.

At first, our captain thought they might come to the ship, but it was impossible to navigate in those high waves.

The days at sea passed rapidly with the usual activities - aerobic classes, lectures, bridge, and dance lessons, duplicate bridge, making miniature models of our ship, and at night, entertainment featuring the passengers and crew.

Everyone was on deck for our early arrival in Buenos Aires. Four years ago, our Norwegian freighter had dropped anchor there. At the American Club, we had made friends with a local couple, the O'Gradys, whom we had written about our arrival, but had no answer in return. To our surprise and delight, they were on the dock to greet us!

They would join us after we returned from an excursion on the Tigre River. Our bus took us through a residential area we hadn't seen before, and then we boarded our launch to sail down the river to a restaurant where we would have lunch. As it was Sunday, we passed many small craft, some of them kayaks, sculls, and rowboats. The homes along the river ranged from mansions to weekend cottages, and all the lawns were well kept.

Our destination, the Gato Blanco (White Cat) was an attractive restaurant, and our meal was delicious.

Later on the ship, we greeted our friends, and took them on a tour of our ship. When we entered the Norway Lounge, our English dance team, Dawn and Alan, were practicing the Argentine Tango. Isabel knows the intricate steps and danced with Alan. It was a treat for her and us, too.

We hated to say goodbye, wondering if we'd see one another again. Our South American friends stayed on the dock waving until our ship was out to sea.

Montevideo is a small country we specially liked because the people are friendly and very artistic. The shop, Manos de Uraquay, welcomed us. Here we found handicrafts made locally. The wind chimes, made of carved gourds, are unusual. As it was very hot, we returned to the ship for lunch.

Everyone was excited about arriving in Rio three days later. We arose at daybreak, and as I pushed back our window curtains, I exclaimed, "There's Bread Loaf!" (I meant Sugar Loaf). The massive rock was pink as the sun rose. Entering the spectacular harbor, we sailed past the "Green Palace" once used by the monarchy and now a military post and found our berth beside a downtown pier. Harry reminded me how our freighter had had to wait six hours before finding a place to leave its cargo.

Before long we were in a cable car riding up Sugar Loaf to its peak. From the summit, the city spreads out along the wide harbor, much of it polluted, so there is little swimming and boating. This day there was so much smog we couldn't see clearly. The park surrounding the mountain is lovely. Our guide said many climb to the top, but we thought the steep ascent and large boulders would make this difficult.

Corcovado, which means "humpbacked mountain", is twice as high as Sugar Loaf. At the top is Christ the Redeemer standing ninety-eight feet tall with arms outstretched over the bay. Made a monument in 1931, it is surrounded by a lovely park with several waterfalls. Half way up we boarded a cog railroad car and finished the twenty four hundred foot ascent. Harry climbed two hundred steps up to the statue. On our descent, a black goat stopped the railcar, and when the conductor tried to catch him, he ran under the car. Finally he was dislodged and we came down. By now, the lights of the city were on and looking back, we could see the lighted figure of Christ against the sky.

Several jewelry salesmen were on our ship, prior to our arrival in Rio. One sat at our table and persuaded us to see his firm's gem collection. After making sure he knew we weren't going to buy anything, we took the Amsterdam Sauer courtesy car to their showroom. The owner, Mr. Sauer, had a breath-taking display of jewels, rubies, amethysts, sapphires, emeralds, topaz, and diamonds in all sizes. The first display showed how these looked before they were cut and then the beautiful multi-faceted gems.

The store actually had a mine shaft, and they showed how one worker at a time was lowered to dig for the precious stones. The most interesting exhibit was one in which the gem cutter actually shaped the jewels. He had been doing this for twenty-five years! Harry offered to buy me a multistone bracelet for $1200, but I refused because if one travels, good jewelry must be left at home. This visit was very educational, stressing the points one should look for in buying precious stones, listed in a book they gave us.

The part of our trip, from Capetown to Rio, covered 4,838 nautical miles, and 5,564 statute miles.

Thus began our last segment, from Rio to Fort Lauderdale. Salvador, the oldest city in Brazil, was our last stop in South America. Once a beautiful metropolis, wealthy from gold, cocoa, and sugar, its buildings — especially the churches — are richly carved and covered with gold leaf. There are rare tilework, arches and sculpture. In the Largo de Pelourinho, Place of the Pillory, a square in the oldest part of the city, slaves were brought from Africa, tortured, and sold here.

The streets were dirty as were the once handsome buildings - a sad aspect for a city once so beautiful. The increase in population has caused a rise in poverty, and petty crime is rampant. We were cautioned to walk together as a group as there were juvenile gangs in the streets ready to rob anyone walking alone. From the top deck I sketched the city, finding it safer to depict the city at a distance.

Now we will have six days at sea before reaching Bridgetown, Barbados. Our world cruise was winding down, and each activity was now treasured, because soon we'd be leaving the ship.

In Barbados, our tour included a visit to Sam Lord's Castle. Once a plantation, this has been made into a luxurious hotel decorated with Barbados mahogany furniture. Much of the china and many of the portraits are spoils taken from ships wrecked on the rocks by the legendary Sam Lord, who is reported to have hung lamps to lure the vessels onto the shallow reef.

The port is colorful with open air markets and coral stone mansions. Bridgetown is now a hub of tourism. Many cruise ships call here with passengers eager to buy duty free items like watches, cameras, transistor radios, and china. The white beaches make this a tropical paradise where many come for carefree vacations.

Our last port of call was St. Thomas, the liveliest of the three American Virgin Islands. We had spent a week here twenty years ago and now found it much changed. There is a new pier with shops convenient for cruise ship passengers. There are still open sided busses loaded with tourists, but the bizarre names are gone, and so are the native sailing ships loaded with produce berthed next to the main dock.

The Danish influence is still evident. The houses in Charlotte Amalie are pastel colored, the cobbled streets narrow and designated by the Danish "Gade" for street. Bluebeard's Castle still serves a good lunch, topped off with a banana daiquiri, and the view of Charlotte Amalie is splendid.

Writers like Herman Wouk, who wrote *Don't Stop the Carnival* here and the great impressionist painter, Camille Pissaro, whose birthplace is on Main Street, were attracted by this scenic island. The interisland boats add to the excitement by coming in at dusk or early morning to unload their baskets of produce on the waterfront sea wall.

Many cruise ships converge on this little seaport sometimes causing a tourist jam in the shops. As in Barbados, duty-free items are much in demand.

Reluctantly, we sailed away realizing our next landing would be in Fort Lauderdale, reluctant because this had been an exciting adventure that was soon to end. However, we were also glad that we were Americans and living in such a country that offers so much in freedom, opportunity, and education. It would be great to be home again and resume living among friends and neighbors with the knowledge that many in the world have so little.

What interesting places we'd visited and what wonderful friends we had made!

Can you believe our voyage from Ft. Lauderdale to Ft. Lauderdale covered 35,619 nautical miles/ 40,961 statute miles? We had visited four continents, Asia, Africa, Australia, and South America, and crossed three oceans, the Pacific, Indian, and Atlantic. Our ship's route had taken us across the Equator six times. There were ninety passengers who sailed around the world, and on various segments about 260, a low number because of Desert Storm that began while we were at sea and ended before we returned.

## About the Author

In her many travels, June Lyman has been able to use her two talents, writing and sketching. She was born in Hinsdale, Illinois, where she spent a happy childhood. Later, she went east to attend Smith College where she majored in art. For a graduation present, her grandmother, Mrs. Charles H. Betts, included her on a six week tour of Europe. The next year, a college friend and she spent three months traveling on an Italian tramp steamer through the Mediterranean.

When June married Harry Lyman, she began an odyssey that has included every kind of travel.

Following artists and where their work is exhibited often determines where the Lymans may go.

In her first book, *Don't Take Away My Paintbrush,* June Lyman reveals her innermost thoughts about art shows, awards and critics. She wrote this especially to encourage anyone to draw and paint.

Once she had two careers: One as a Girl Scout Field Director and then as an assistant editor in Language Arts, Scott Foresman Publishing Company.

Both Lyman's daughters acquired their mother's love of writing and painting. Barbara died in 1976 but her sister, Sally, carries on the family talent by being a Vermont newspaper editor and free-lance writer.

Recently, the Lymans returned from a world cruise where June sketched at all thirty-one ports-of-call and had an art exhibit just before arriving in Capetown. When not hanging pictures, Harry was forming a barbershop quartet to entertain the passengers.

Although now in her seventies, June Lyman looks forward to their next trip and already dreams of a cruise in the eastern Mediterranean.

Which mode of travel does she prefer? This is a question often asked. "A week or more stay in a foreign country is more relaxing than being continually on the move," she says. All she needs is for Harry to say, "Are you ready to go?" and she begins to pack. New adventures, new friends, new horizons make for an exciting life. But, even without these, there are her diaries, picture albums and videos of trips already taken to awaken memories. In addition are her sketchbooks with scenes to be painted. All she needs, June Lyman sighs, is more hours in the day for all she wants to do.